THE SELDEN MAP OF CHINA

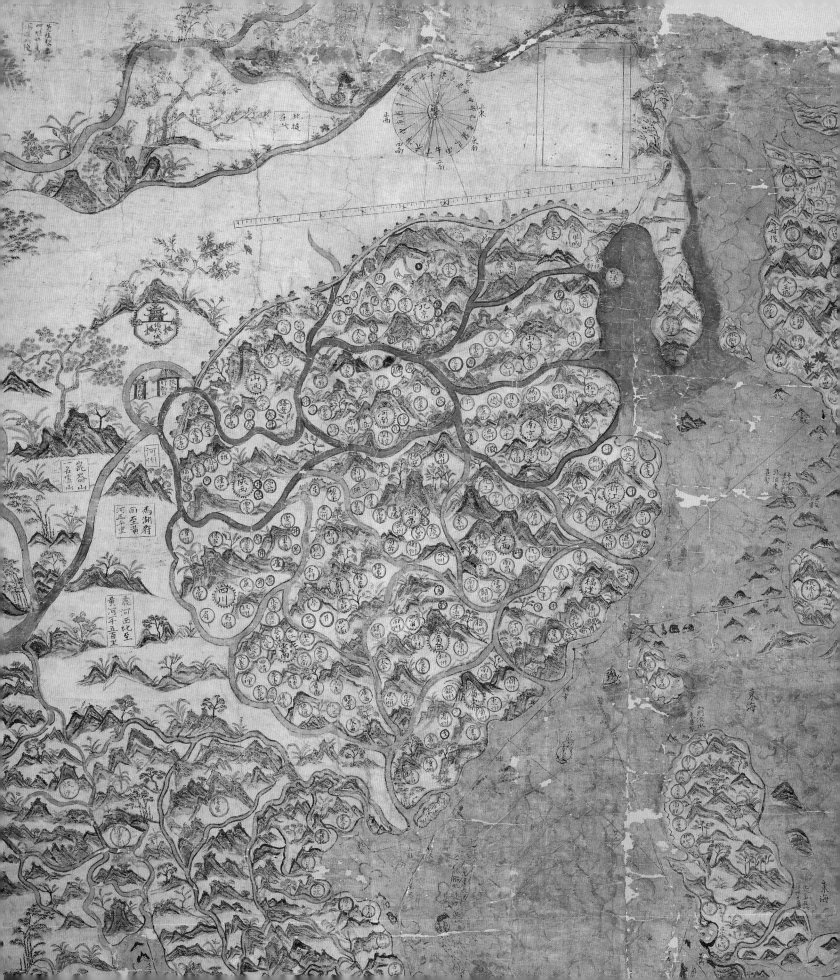

THE SELDEN MAP OF CHINA
A New Understanding of the Ming Dynasty

HONGPING ANNIE NIE

Bodleian Library
UNIVERSITY OF OXFORD

To Juliana

First published in 2019 by the Bodleian Library
Broad Street, Oxford OX1 3BG
www.bodleianshop.co.uk

ISBN 978 1 85124 524 6

Text © Hongping Annie Nie, 2019

All images, unless specified,
© Bodleian Library, University of Oxford, 2019

Hongping Nie has asserted her right to be
identified as the author of this Work.

Cover design by Dot Little at the Bodleian Library
Designed and typeset in 12½ on 16 Perpetua by illuminati, Grosmont
Printed and bound by Printer Trento on 150 gsm Gardamatt Art paper

British Library Catalogue in Publishing Data
A CIP record of this publication is available from the British Library

CONTENTS

A DISCOVERY IN THE LIBRARY

Early on the morning of 10 January 2008, Robert Batchelor, an American historian from Georgia Southern University, arrived at the Bodleian Library. Located in the heart of Oxford, the Bodleian, founded in 1602, is the central library of the University of Oxford and stores 8.5 million of the University's 13 million books. It is not only the largest university library in Europe but also one of the continent's largest national libraries.

Batchelor would come to Oxford every January to attend the annual conference of the British Society for Eighteenth-Century Studies, and at the same time would visit the Bodleian's premodern East Asian collection. Scheduled to fly back to the United States the next day, he decided to make another visit to the Bodleian to have a look at a Chinese map from the Ming dynasty listed as 'The Selden map of China' in the library's catalogue (the map had no title on it; following a seventeenth-century tradition, it had been named after John

Selden (1584–1654), who had donated it to the library). Batchelor had not the slightest idea that he was about to make a historical discovery.

David Helliwell, curator of the Bodleian's Chinese collections, met with Batchelor in one of the reading rooms. He brought out the rarely used Selden map from storage and carefully spread it out on a big table. The old map, 158 cm long and 96 cm wide, was seriously damaged in many places. Its original colours were badly faded; it exuded the distinctive odour of ancient book collections. As he had hoped, Batchelor identified it as an original map from the Ming dynasty (1368–1644). However, to his amazement, the map in front of him was completely different from any other Chinese map he had ever seen. Unlike typical ancient Chinese maps, which placed China at the centre of the world and scattered other countries as little pieces of territory around the periphery, the Selden map of China covered vast areas of ocean

1 The Selden map of China (MS. Selden supra 105), created between the late sixteenth and early seventeenth centuries

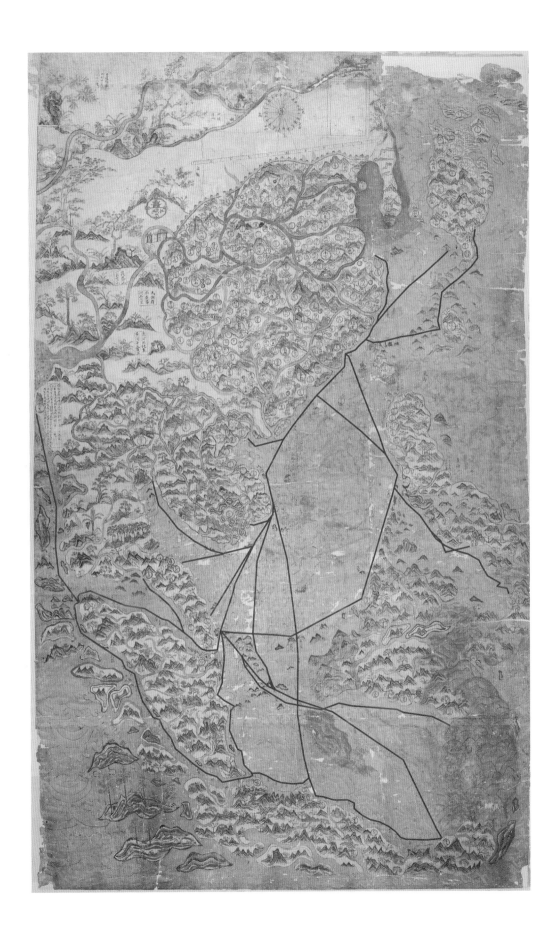

2 Trading routes shown on the Selden map

3 The Selden map of China before conservation, rolled

and islands. It stretched from Siberia in the north to Java and the Moluccas (the Spice Islands) in the south. To the east of the map were the islands of Japan and the Philippines; to the west were Burma and southern India, with instructions for reaching the Persian Gulf (Hormuz) and the Red Sea (Aden). Interestingly, mainland China was squeezed into the upper left part of the map, while the islands of East Asia and South East Asia occupied more than half its total area. Although each Chinese administrative district was outlined with a thick green line, and the names of each province, prefecture, and county were systematically marked, Batchelor noticed that there were few other details about the inland areas.

In the soft light of the reading room, Batchelor also noticed a number of scarcely discernible thin black lines linking the Fujian coast with various ports in East and South East Asia, and almost unnoticeable navigation markings next to the lines. His many years of research into the history of world trade had given him exceptional insight. He immediately realized that these lines were none other than Ming dynasty trade routes. The so-called 'Selden map of China' actually depicted the seafaring routes known to the merchants of Ming China. Batchelor was delighted with his discovery, for he knew what a great impact it would have on the world's knowledge of Ming China. The image of an isolated and conservative China during the Ming dynasty in conventional scholarship was wrong; here instead was evidence that Ming China was outward-looking and capitalistic. Turning to Helliwell, Batchelor exclaimed: 'This map will become world famous. It will appear in all the history textbooks!'[1]

News of Batchelor's discovery quickly spread through academic circles around the world. Experts agreed that the map was an extremely significant Chinese historical document which forced a re-assessment of the relationship between marine and inland China during the Ming dynasty and of the position of the Ming dynasty in the world.

Chinese academics now commonly refer to the map as the Nautical Chart of the Eastern and Western Seas (東西洋航海圖), a title that is included in the Bodleian Library's catalogue.

4 The Selden map of China before conservation

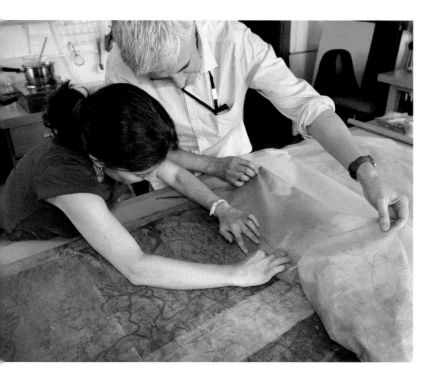

5 Removal of the early-twentieth-century textile lining

6 Conservators infilling losses with dyed Chinese paper

The Selden map of China had been kept in a long box, where it had become seriously damaged from being rolled up too tightly. It would be taken out to show to visitors as a Chinese curiosity, and by the beginning of the twentieth century was badly worn. In 1919, employing contemporary methods of conservation, it had been backed with textile, which proved to be an unfortunate mistake. As time passed, the backing stiffened and each time the map was opened and unrolled fragments of the map dropped off, causing further damage.

Immediately after the rediscovery of the Selden map of China, Robert Minte and Marinita Stiglitz submitted a proposal to conserve it. The Pilgrim Trust, the Radcliffe Trust and the Mercers' Company generously provided funding, which enabled the Bodleian Library's conservation team, led by Robert Minte, to take on the task of conservation.

CONSERVING THE MAP

This became one of the most challenging conservation projects the Bodleian conservators had ever encountered. After several months of careful consideration they finalized their conservation plan. They decided to combine techniques and materials from East and West to conserve the map and preserve all of its material characteristics and historical evidence,

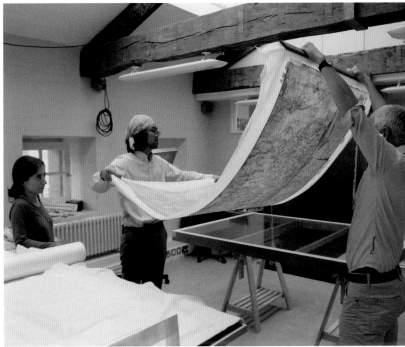

7 Removal of temporary facing prior to relining

8 The Selden map during the relining process

while removing the century-old lining and repairs. Removing the textile lining and older paper patches from the back proved to be the most difficult part of the project, a painstaking process which took several months. The conservators first gradually humidified the surface from both sides using dahlia sprayers and Japanese brushes in order to enable the textile lining to be removed, to flatten distortions and to draw out discolouration. They then used Japanese paste brushes to apply a temporary facing on the front, adhered with Japanese red seaweed extract, while the textile backing was being removed. The backing had been stuck on with strong adhesive and the paper of the map was extremely thin and fragile.

They had to use special bamboo utensils to carefully remove the backing and patches bit by bit.

After the backing was successfully removed, they used Chinese dyed paper to fill in damaged areas and applied three layers of Japanese paper to the back of the map in order to strengthen it. At different stages of the conservation they brought in experts with special skills from the British Museum and the British Library to help them. As a result, a year later the map had regained much of its original beautiful appearance. In September 2011 the map made its debut at the *Treasures of the Bodleian* exhibition, revealing its splendour to the world and becoming a great attraction.

A CARTOGRAPHIC WORK OF ART

The Selden map of China is a work of art, beautifully painted in multiple colours and black Chinese carbon ink on three pieces of *Mitsumata* paper, made from the Japanese plant of that name (*Edgeworthia chrysantha*), which was cultivated in China and Korea in the seventeenth century and widely traded. It is a large map, measuring 158 cm in length by 96 cm in width. It is too big to have been conveniently employed as a chart. Most likely it would have been used to decorate a wealthy merchant's house, hung on the wall as a display of its owner's maritime knowledge, connections and power. The central point of the map is the middle of the South China Sea. It extends from Siberia to Java and Indonesia and the Moluccas; from the islands of Japan and the Philippines to Burma and southern India. In the foreground, more than sixty ports are labelled along the shipping routes, as well as countries, Japanese provinces, islands, reefs, rivers, mountains and ocean currents. At the top of the map are a compass rose, a scale bar and an empty rectangular bordered box. A box on the western edge of the map gives directions for reaching the Persian Gulf and the Red Sea. There is an image of the sun on the upper right edge of the map and an image of the moon at the upper west end of the map. As an analysis of the ink used has revealed, the Latin words for sun and moon are written on each respective image in the handwriting of Thomas Hyde, Bodley's Librarian 1665–1701, who made several inscriptions on the map in collaboration with Shen Fuzong, a scholar from China.

The clear focus of the Selden map is China's coastal regions and islands from north to south, as well as the eastern and western oceanic regions. The Chinese mainland is squeezed into the upper left part of the map; it is rather distorted in shape and situated in a less important position. Each Ming dynasty administrative area is outlined with a thick green line. The names of each province, seat of

9 (*opposite and overleaf*) Details of the sun and moon on the Selden map of China

government, prefecture and county are marked with different signs, but there are few details about the inland areas. Japan and the Korean Peninsula are just sketched in and are not very accurate. However, the depiction of the topography of South East Asia is relatively accurate and the Philippines are drawn in detail, with sixteen names marked. The ocean and islands occupy about half of the map. As a fusion of Chinese cartography and Western cartography, the Selden map represents a major breakthrough in traditional Chinese geographical conceptions.

Above the Malay Peninsula and close to the Indian Ocean, where India is supposed to be, are the 'sources of the Yellow River' (黃河水源) and the 'Constellation Sea' (星宿海), as well as the sources of the Yangtze River and the Mekong River. The river sources here largely follow a mythical understanding of the Himalayan watershed while the maritime information is almost entirely non-mythical. Flowing down the east side, the Kuroshio Current is marked as 'Yegu Passage, eastward current, very tight' (野故門水流東) by Ryukyu and 'This passage, flowing east, extremely tight' (此門流水東甚緊) between Taiwan and Luzon.

The Selden map shows considerable contemporary geographical and nautical knowledge. It marks six eastern sea routes and twelve western sea routes of Chinese boats sailing from Quanzhou (泉州) on the Fujian coast as well as sixty ports along these routes. There are also characters written next to the routes, indicating the compass directions for their main stages. Although the map extends only as

10 (*opposite*) A warning about strong currents around Quanzhou on the Selden map of China

far west as the Bay of Bengal, on the far left of the chart, near Calicut (古裡國), is a text explaining the route to Aden (阿丹國), Dhofar (法兒國) and Hormuz (忽魯謨茲), which demonstrates Ming China's knowledge of and interest in the Persian Gulf and the Red Sea regions.

The cartographer who drew the Selden map used Chinese landscape painting techniques, sketching in ink the outline of mountain ranges, forests, plants and flowers, rivers, ocean waves, and so on, and then applying six different colours – red, green, blue, yellow, white and black. Particular topographical features, such as mountains, rivers, islands and straits, provincial boundaries, cities and coastal maritime routes are shown in different colours and patterns. A nautical chart, the Selden map can also be appreciated as a beautiful landscape painting, a perfect combination of the two forms.

It is clear that whoever created the Selden map had considerable knowledge of South East Asia's landscape and local products. The map depicts different species of trees, whose growth patterns roughly correspond to the longitude, including cedar, plum, willow, bamboo, camphor, pine and palm. But the trees depicted in Ming territory are not the same as those depicted in the tropics of South East Asia. On the island east of Sumatra are images of different kinds of palm trees used as cash crops. Many other plants are shown on the map, including orchids, peonies and loquats, some repeatedly. In the south of Japan a scarlet chrysanthemum flower is painted (13).

11 Plants and landscape on the Selden map of China

12 A wood depicted on the Selden map of China

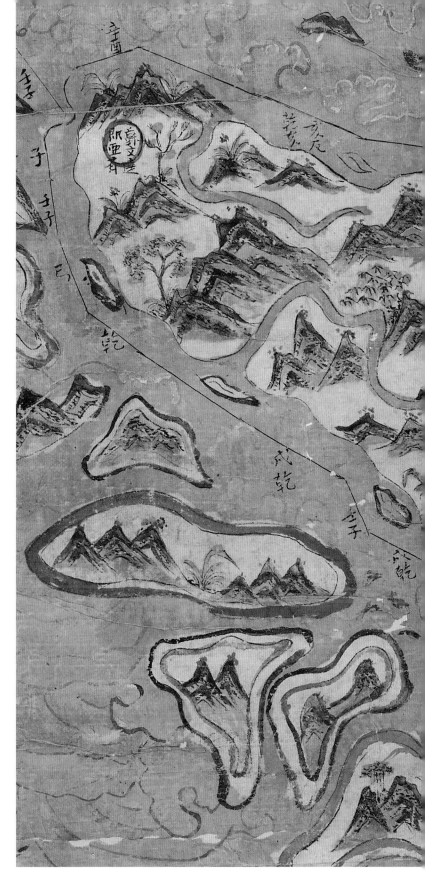

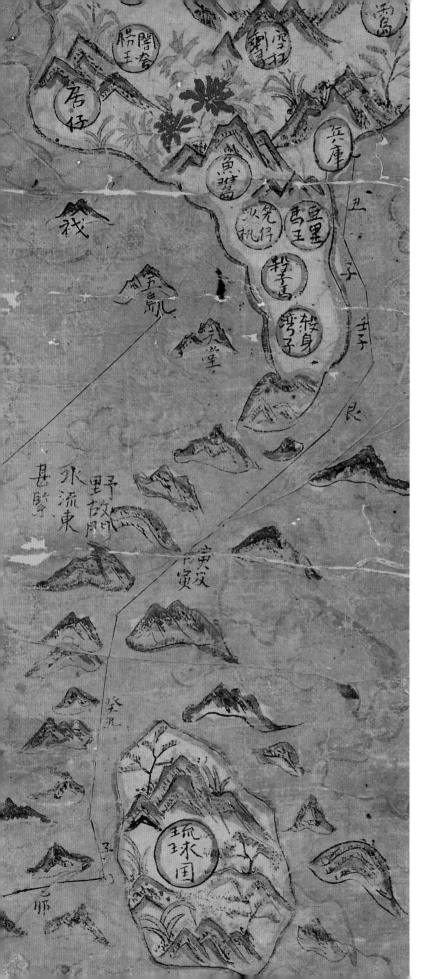

CHINESE CARTOGRAPHY

Cartography in ancient China was closely associated with the concept of the 'world under heaven' (天下觀) and the idea of barbarians (華夷觀).[2] The 'world under heaven' referred to the territories that might be reached by the power of the emperor, with China seen as the centre of the world and of civilization. The further out from the centre in all four directions, the more barbaric the world became. The map of the 'world under heaven' and the map of the 'world of barbarians' are the same, the latter simply being an extension of the former. As a result, the traditional Chinese cartographic method was to position China in the centre, with tiny areas of foreign land scattered around the periphery. Jesuit missionary Matteo Ricci's geographical concepts influenced a group of Chinese scholars, but the world maps made by the traditional literati were still Sinocentric. For example, in 1644 Cao Junyi (曹君義) drew a world map entitled 'A Complete Map of the Nine Border Towns, Allotted Fields, Human Presence, and Travel Routes of All under Heaven' (天下九邊分野人跡 路程全圖). He depicted with some accuracy the geographical positions of Europe, the Mediterranean and Africa, but Europe and America were still shown as tiny areas of barbarian land in the west. Around the huge Chinese territory was a partitioned and caricaturized Western-style world map. The lines of longitude and latitude on Cao's world map, which did not appear on the Selden map, were mere decoration.[3] Although the author of the Selden map

13 Red chrysanthemums painted on Japan on the Selden map of China

14 A map of China and neighbouring countries (*Tianxa jiubian fenye renji luchen quantu*), by Cao Junyi, 1644

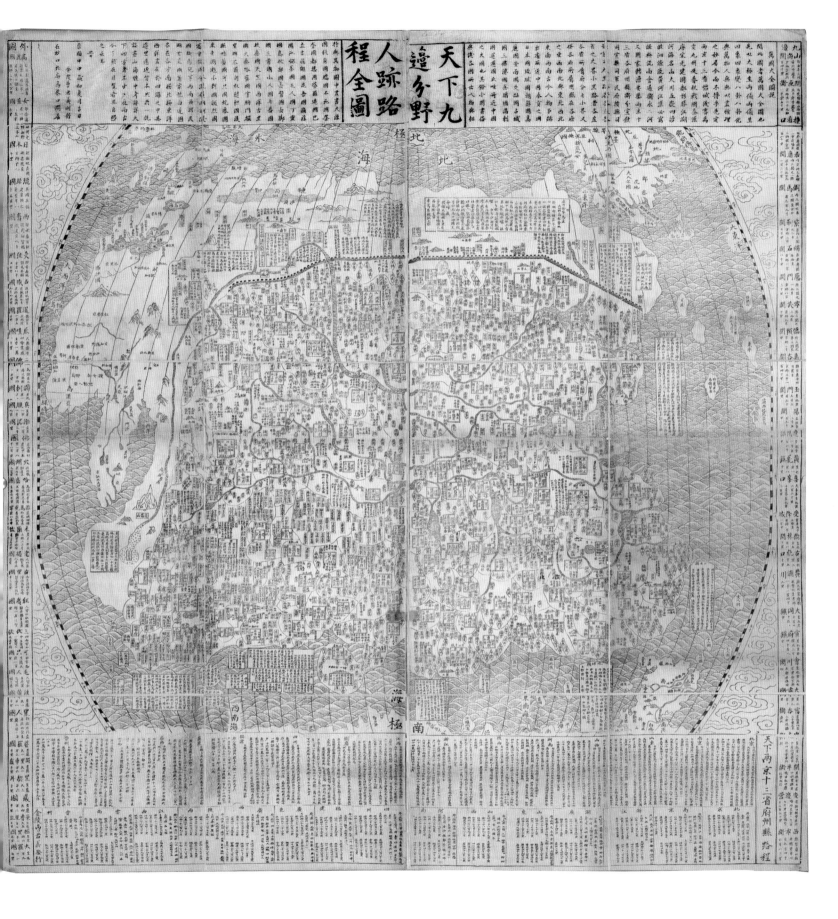

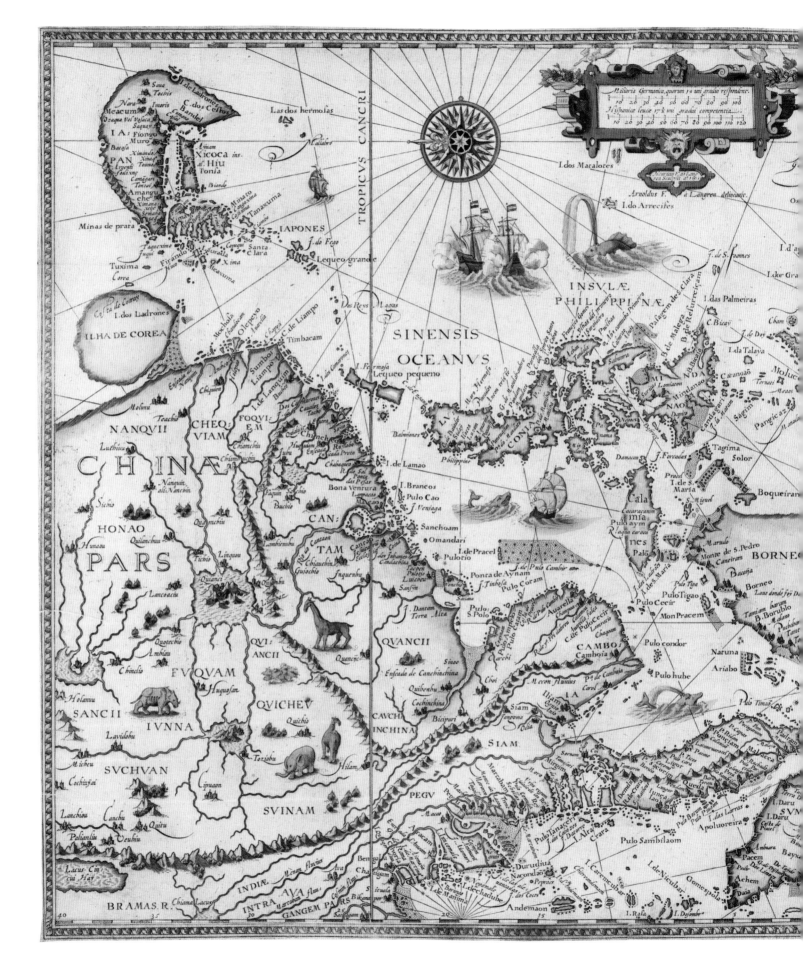

made India small and only provided inscriptions in the upper left indicating the Netherlands and England, China was no longer treated as the centre of the world as in traditional Chinese cartography.

In ancient Chinese cartography the seas were marginalized.[4] Although Ming sea maps, such as those in the map collection entitled *Chou hai tu bian* (籌海图编, *Sea Maps Collection*), show the topography of Chinese and foreign lands, cities and towns, rivers and islands, and coastal defences, almost all were official maps made for national defence purposes or imperial envoys sent abroad on diplomatic missions. Despite China's long seafaring history, Chinese nautical charts that have survived to the present day are extremely rare.

The Zheng He Nautical Chart, also called Mao Kun Map (鄭和航海圖), is the only nautical chart of the high seas that has survived from the Ming dynasty. In the early Ming dynasty (from 1405 until 1433), Zheng He was asked by the Ming emperor to lead seven ocean expeditions to South East Asia, India, the Persian Gulf and the east coast of Africa to demonstrate Ming power. Based on Zheng He's expeditions, the Zheng He Nautical Chart consists of forty small charts as printed in the *Sea Maps Collection* (籌海圖編). It includes eighteen charts of China and twenty-two charts of foreign parts, as well as two pages of seafaring constellation charts. The Zheng He Nautical Chart shows fifty-six compass course routes from Taicang in Jiangsu to Hormuz and fifty-three return routes, depicting in Chinese landscape-painting style the different scenery along

15 Sixteenth-century map of China, Japan, Korea, South East Asia, the Philippines, the Straits of Malacca, Borneo, Java and Beach, engraved by Robert Beckit for John Wolfe's English translation of Linschoten's *Itinerario* (1596)

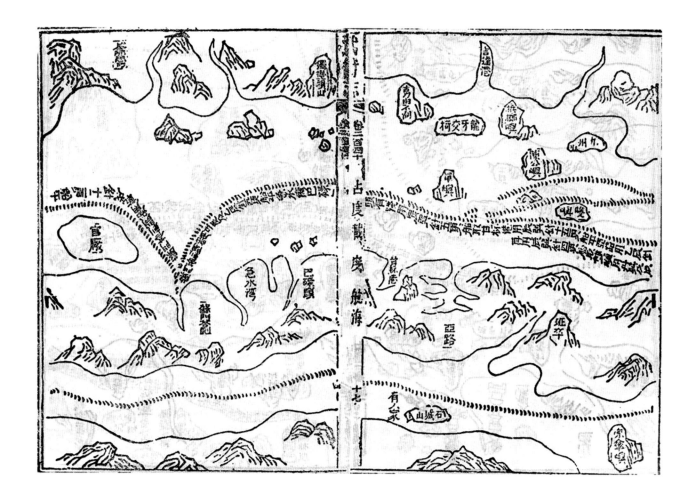

16 Zhen He Nautical Chart, 1620

17 Dutch population described on the Selden map of China

the Yangtze River below Nanjing, the East China Sea and the South Sea as far as the Indian Ocean, the Persian Gulf, East African routes and the coastal terrain.

While the Zheng He Nautical Chart is evidence of state-sponsored tributary navigation taking place in early Ming, the Selden map records the commercial voyages of late Ming merchants who ventured into maritime trade despite the Ming court's ban. The Selden map of China shows not only China within its borders but also the world that lies beyond, especially the open seas. As a merchant map, the Selden map not only highlights the importance of the trading activities of ordinary merchants, but also reflects a new type of relationship between merchants and the state, the world and the oceans in Ming China.

Typical of later Chinese traditional nautical charts, the Zheng He Nautical Chart lacks a compass rose or scale. In traditional Chinese

nautical charts the topographical features were vividly depicted so that map users could identify their location by matching their surroundings with a particular scene on the chart – the 'scene-matching method' (對景法). With this placing of the user in a central position, the compass was not a factor. The scale was not necessarily consistent, while lines and text are relied upon for explanation. In contrast, Western portolan charts typically featured many radial navigation lines, a compass rose and a scale, which helped the voyager determine the orientation of his ship on the ocean and the distance to the destination. The coastal areas were depicted in more detail while land areas were either left blank or filled with images. These charts were typically painted on parchment paper less than 1 metre square and sometimes several charts formed a set of maps.

The Selden map is the first Chinese map that correctly shows the geographical relationships in the East Asia region. It depicts China as being a part of East and South East Asia. China is shown merged into the region and not dominating this part of the world. Such a large-scale depiction of the oceans on a single map is a feature of the Western Ptolemaic method of looking at the world on a single chart. It shows at a glance China's global position in Asia's seas and oceans and the main routes connecting Ming China to the world. More importantly, with Europeans marked on the map – Spanish, English, Dutch – the Selden map indicates a strong sense of dynamic global encounter. It is possible that contemporary Western world maps may have been consulted by the cartographer.

The Selden map, made two hundred years after the Zheng He Nautical Chart, is the first map to

mark compass bearings and scale. It clearly displays an unusually strong sense of direction and distance. In the centre of the upper part of the Selden map is a traditional Chinese mariner's compass rose, accurately showing eight points of the compass: east, west, north, south, south-east, south-west, north-east and north-west. Furthermore, on the route to Ryukyu each stage is marked with compass bearings, respectively: 甲卯 (85°), 乙卯 (95°), 卯 (90°), 乙卯 (95°), 卯 (90°), 乙卯 (95°), and so on. However, the Selden map incorporates the scenery elements of the traditional 'scene-matching method' as used in the Zheng He Nautical Chart. For example, along the route through the South China Sea, there are clearly islands and rivers that are markers indicating where to turn and where to take a bearing.

Below the compass rose on the Selden map is a slightly slanted scale. Some believe that the map-maker did not understand how scale was used for guided navigation and added it to the map as a decoration in reference to some contemporary Western nautical charts; others believe that it could indeed be a Chinese type of nautical scale: 1 inch (寸) equivalent to a voyage of ten night watches (更, geng). According to ancient Chinese ways of calculating time, one day was ten night watches, and one night watch was equal to 2.4 hours. In Ming China the geng was already being used as a unit of measurement in maritime navigation. In the space of one geng, a vessel travelling at normal speed could cover an average of 60 miles. For example, the sea route from Manila to Brunei on modern maps is a distance of 1,185 km (640 nautical miles). According to the

18 Detail of the compass rose and scale bar on the Selden map of China. The mysterious blank rectangle can also be seen

scale on the Selden map this would take a voyage of 6.2 days, or 62 geng; in other words 4.3 nautical miles per hour. Based on original navigational data, this speed is fairly accurate.[5]

The blank rectangle to the right of the compass rose and above the scale is more intriguing. Some believe it is an unfinished part of the map; others think it represents the map itself, and that the combination of the slanted scale and the blank rectangle indicates the magnetic declination of the map – that is, the map conveyed not only a 'compass north' but also a 'map north'.[6] However, magnetic declination was not well understood across the world at the beginning of the seventeenth century and there was no credible evidence to support the claim that the discrepancy shown between the scale and the rectangular frame of the Selden map was China's magnetic declination at the time.

SHIPPING ROUTES

During conservation, after the backing and patches had been removed, it was found that on the back of the Selden map was a sketch of a scale, navigation points and a diagram showing the shipping routes. The discovery of this sketch confirms that the shipping routes are the focus of the Selden map. Most likely the map was constructed by combining the routes on the back of the map with a portolan-style chart. The trunk route ran parallel to the coast of Fujian, starting from Goto Island (五島) off Nagasaki (籠仔沙機) and Hirado (魚鱗島) in Japan, through Quanzhou (泉州) in Chinese coastal province Fujian (福建), towards Hui An (會安) and Champa (占城) in central Vietnam, and finally reaching Pahang (彭坊) on the Malay Peninsula. It was the route of Japanese silver going out, along the Chinese coast and down to Vietnam, Siam and the Malay Peninsula, where Chinese merchants came to trade with goods such as silk and ceramics.

In addition to the trunk route, the Selden map records a network of routes, starting from Quanzhou, stretching from Nagasaki south to Timor and Sumatra, the so-called eastern and western routes at the time. These trading routes 'witnessed heavy traffic in the early seventeenth century from Chinese merchants, Japanese red seal ships and the Dutch East India Company and the British East India Company'.[7] The Selden map is of great significance for research into international trade in East and South East Asia during the Ming dynasty, especially the relationship between China and the galleon trade, as well as the important role China played in the emergence of global trade in the early modern period.

19 The back of the Selden Map of China after removal of the textile lining, showing a sketch of scale, navigation points and a diagram of shipping routes

THE HISTORY OF THE SELDEN MAP

It is widely accepted that the Selden map of China was created between the late sixteenth and the early seventeenth century, at the end of the Ming dynasty's Wanli era and the beginning of the Tianqi era, when maritime trade with foreign countries was flourishing after the Ming court lifted its ban on foreign trade. Some scholars, basing their theory on the evidence of changes in Taiwan's name, believe that the Selden map was created in the Wanli era between 1566 and 1602.[8] Others, extrapolating from contemporary terms of address used by the Dutch, the Spanish and the Portuguese, believe it is most likely that the map was produced between 1610 and 1620.[9] However, others assert that the map was created at the earliest in the sixth year of the Wanli era (1578), and that it was probably produced around 1621 after the Dutch occupied the Moluccas (present-day Indonesia), before they entered Tainan (in Taiwan), in 1624, around the fourth year of the Tianqi era.[10]

The creator of the Selden map of China is unknown; experts have made many suggestions regarding their identity. Some believe it likely that the creator was from southern Fujian, as the starting points of all the sea routes, whether eastern or western, are along the south-east coast of Fujian, and many of the characters on the map are written in the southern Fujian vernacular. Others suggest that the map-maker was a sinicized Arab who had settled in Fujian, because the map provides directions to Arab regions in the Middle East.[11] The creator could alternatively have been a Chinese resident of the Philippines because the term for the Spanish in the inscription by the Moluccas, 化人, is what Chinese people in the Philippines called the Spaniards.[12] On the other hand, given that Spanish, Portuguese and Dutch were active in South East Asia, the map could also have been the result of an encounter between China and the West.[13]

20 Instructions for navigating to the Persian Gulf and Red Sea on the left-hand side of the Selden map of China

How the Selden map travelled far across the seas from China or South East Asia to England is a mystery. One theory is connected with Banten on the island of Java, the biggest pepper trading centre in South East Asia at the beginning of the seventeenth century, which attracted merchants from Europe, South West Asia, South China, the Malay Peninsula and the Spice Islands. Fujian merchants and the British East India Company were the most active, and the two sides would often cooperate in managing the pepper purchasing and exporting business. It is possible that at the beginning of the seventeenth century an English person with the British East India Company in Banten might have obtained the map from a Fujianese pepper merchant and later taken it back to London.[14]

Another theory is that the East India Company commander John Saris, captain of the first British ship to reach Japan and a significant figure, might have accepted the map in lieu of a large trading debt.[15]

Batchelor proposes a different theory. He suggests that the Selden map of China, which he believes was commissioned by Li Dan (d. 1625), the most powerful Chinese merchant at the time, was on a ship to Japan and became one of the spoils of war when the English and the Dutch jointly enforced a blockade on Portuguese trade in the region.[16] Li Dan was the leader of China's biggest merchant group and was known by foreigners as Captain China. He had a close relationship with the Japanese upper classes and also cooperated in trade with Richard Cocks of the British East India Company. Every year his smuggling ships would sail back and forth between Japan, China and Taiwan in the South China Sea. It is suggested that one of Li Dan's ships sailed from Manila via Macau back to Nagasaki.

The captain was registered under the name of an Osaka merchant and the crew was made up of Chinese, Japanese and Portuguese. There were also two Portuguese priests disguised as merchants, who were preparing to slip into Japan to do missionary work. Japan at that time prohibited trade with Portugal and Spain, both Catholic countries. Supported by the Japanese government, Britain and the Netherlands jointly imposed a blockade on Portuguese and Spanish ships entering Japan. A British East India Company ship, *The Elizabeth*, had just arrived from London and was keen to prevent the Portuguese Catholic missionaries from doing their work. It intercepted and seized Li Dan's ship near Taiwan. It was purely by chance that the Nautical Chart of the Eastern and Western Seas happened to be on this ship.

This incident had disastrous consequences in Nagasaki. Li Dan was suspected of illegally transporting Portuguese missionaries into Japan as well as smuggling goods. In order to protect their own companies, he and Richard Cocks tried to deflect public attention away from the smuggling and onto the missionaries. Li Dan was able to escape, but the Japanese captain and two Portuguese priests were tortured and put to death. This became a notorious case of martyrdom in the history of Catholicism. The British and Dutch blockade was finally lifted, but a great quantity of Li Dan's merchandise was confiscated and Richard Cocks died in disgrace on the journey back to England.

Nevertheless, there is no hard evidence to confirm that the Selden map of China fell into

21 John Selden (1584–1654), who bequeathed the map to the Bodleian Library, painted c. 1708

the hands of the British during this blockade. East India Company archives have always been preserved intact, but surprisingly the record of the blockade by *The Elizabeth* is missing. Many of the materials, including the papers of the most experienced English chart-maker in Japan at the time, Gabriel Tatton, were scattered and lost after reaching London. Since there is no record, one can only speculate about what happened. The mystery remains unsolved.

The Selden map was later acquired by John Selden, a well-known London lawyer and Oriental scholar educated at the University of Oxford. Selden described the map in a codicil to his will dated 11 June 1653:

> A map of China made there fairly, and done in colours, together with a sea compass of their making and divisions, taken both by an English commander, who being pressed exceedingly to restore it at a great ransom, would not part with it.[17]

In his will Selden said that he hoped to donate the map and other items in his collection, including many oriental manuscripts and Greek marble carvings, to a public library.

John Selden composed a treatise in 1619 (revised and published in 1635) entitled *Mare Clausum* ('The Closed Sea'), in response to a similar book, *Mare Liberum* ('The Open Sea') by the Dutch scholar Hugo Grotius. Grotius asserted that the seas were shared internationally and that any country could freely engage in all maritime trade. But Selden

22 Duke Humfrey's Library, Oxford. The 'Selden End', an extension to the original library named after John Selden, who donated 8,000 items, was completed in 1640

believed that sea (dominion) is not the same as land/territory (sovereignty). He would prohibit the Dutch from expanding into the North Sea and he also opposed the joint British and Dutch blockade of the Portuguese sea route at Manila. That Selden had the map in his collection clearly arose from his great interest in maritime rights and trade. If the map was really one of the spoils of war from concerted action taken by the British and the Dutch, then the fact that it had fallen into his hands was indeed an irony.

THE BODLEIAN LIBRARY

John Selden died in 1654, and in 1659 the map was presented to the Bodleian Library. The Bodleian has a long tradition of collecting Chinese books and manuscripts. As early as 1604, the University alumnus, diplomat and promoter of knowledge Thomas Bodley purchased for the Library a batch of Chinese books from Amsterdam, Europe's largest oriental commodities transit station, although at the time no English or Dutch scholars could read Chinese. Throughout the seventeenth century the Bodleian acquired Europe's biggest collection of Chinese works, around a fifth of Europe's entire Chinese book collection. Fortunately almost all have survived.[18]

Thomas Hyde (1636–1703), an Oriental scholar and librarian-in-chief at the Bodleian Library, was not able to catalogue the Chinese book collection, which included the Selden map, until 1687, the year in which he met a visitor from China. Shen Fuzong (Michael Alphonsius, 1657–1692) was a Chinese Catholic who, in 1683, had accompanied the Belgian Jesuit Philippe Couplet (1623–1693) to Rome to give an account of missionary work in China to the Pope. Along the way, Shen Fuzong

was received by the French king, Louis XIV, to whom he showed a portrait of Confucius and demonstrated calligraphy with a writing brush. This visit facilitated the sending of the first group of French missionaries to China in 1685. Couplet and Shen Fuzong went once again to Rome for an audience with Pope Innocent XI and offered him more than 400 scrolls compiled by missionaries and edited from Chinese documents; these formed an early collection of Chinese books in the Vatican library. In 1687 Couplet and Shen Fuzong paid a formal visit to the English king, James II. James took a great liking to this knowledgeable Chinese man and asked the artist Sir Godfrey Kneller to paint a full, life-size portrait of Shen Fuzong, which he hung in his bedroom.

In the summer of 1687 Hyde invited Shen Fuzong to Oxford to help translate the titles of Chinese books and manuscripts into Latin and compile a catalogue. In a letter to a friend, Hyde wrote: 'Michael Shen Fuzong is a scholar well-versed in all areas of Chinese learning, and is sincere and dependable ..., he can speak Latin and we can freely communicate.' In the accounts of the Bodleian Library for the years 1686 and 1687 a disbursement of £6 can be seen: 'Payment to the Chinese man for cataloguing Chinese books and other expenses and board and lodging.'[19] With Shen Fuzong's help, Thomas Hyde added Latin notes on the Selden map, which we can still see today. In 1688 Shen Fuzong left Oxford for Lisbon and became a Jesuit. Unfortunately, in 1691 on his way back to China he fell ill and died. His portrait still hangs in Windsor Castle today.

In 1697 the Oxford scholar Edward Bernard (1638–1697) included the Chinese catalogue compiled by Shen Fuzong and Thomas Hyde in the

the famous Latin catalogue *Catalogi librorum manu-scriptorum Angliae et Hiberniae*. Several hundred years later the Bodleian's curator of Chinese Collections, David Helliwell, updated and annotated Edward Bernard's catalogue, which led Robert Batchelor to the rediscovery of the Selden map in 2008.

On 15 September 2011 the University of Oxford organized an international conference on the map, during which scholars from around the world discussed its features and its significance. There was unanimous agreement that the Selden map is an extremely important Chinese historical document. Renowned sinologist Timothy Brook declared it to be the most important Chinese historical document he had ever seen. Zhang Zhiqing (张志清), Head of Special Collections at the National Library of China, believes it to be more important than any of the pre-modern maps in his care.

The collection includes the Laud Rutter (*Shunfeng xiangsong* 順風相送), a Ming navigator's manuscript donated by William Laud (1573–1645), Archbishop of Canterbury 1633–45 and Chancellor of Oxford University 1630–41. It is a late Ming manual of compass directions to the sea routes connecting China to East Asia, South East Asia and South Asia. Each route is broken down into a sequence of compass bearings and the distances over which the pilot should hold to that course until another bearing is given. Some of the compass bearings in the Laud Rutter can be found on the Selden map of China. Obviously the cartography of the Selden map closely matches the written text of the Laud Rutter in terms of describing the established routes.[20]

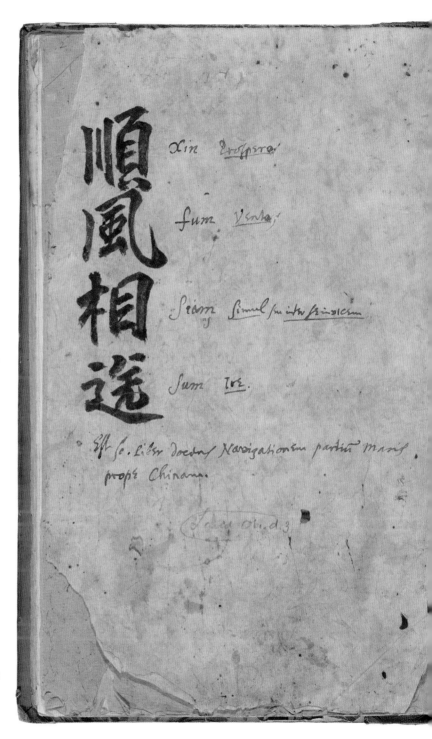

23 Michael Alphonsus Shen Fuzong (*c.* 1658–1691), painted in 1687

24 A late Ming manual of compass directions to the sea routes connecting China with other continents, *Shunfeng xiangsong* ('Favourable Winds in Escort'), MS. Laud Or. 145

MING DYNASTY MARITIME TRADE

The Ming dynasty, which witnessed China's second commercial revolution, was a rather open, dynamic and outward-looking period of Chinese history. Despite the Ming court's ban on maritime trade with foreign countries, overseas trade flourished as never before during this period. The newly discovered Selden map of China reveals Ming China's maritime commercial activities in various coastal ports between the Pacific and the Indian oceans, east to Japan, Korea, via the Philippines and the South Sea Islands, and west to the Arabian Peninsula and as far as the east coast of Africa. Chinese merchants could be seen everywhere.

COMMODITIES, MARITIME NAVIGATION AND SHIPBUILDING TECHNOLOGY

In the reign of the first Ming ruler Emperor Hongwu (1368–1398) China's autocratic, imperial power system was at its height. However, compared to previous dynasties, economic development in the Ming Empire was unprecedented. The Ming dynasty was the pinnacle of Chinese culture with regard to technology, commerce, art and literature.

Emperor Hongwu was born into a peasant family and attached great importance to agriculture. When he ascended to the throne, he immediately resumed the agricultural production that had been destroyed in the late Yuan dynasty. As society stabilized, agricultural production increased, creating considerable surpluses. Infrastructure and communication improved under Emperor Hongwu; private business and trade were also promoted. New markets burgeoned along the route of the messengers of the imperial court, where surplus agricultural commodities were sold in great quantity, ushering in the Ming dynasty's commercial revolution.[21]

China's financial strength and power continued to grow during the Yongle era (1402–24). Emperor Yongle is universally regarded as the Ming dynasty's 'second founding emperor of China', because he

25 *Kraak* porcelain from China, possibly traded by the Dutch East India Company, *c.* 1600–1624

26 A marketplace in prosperous Nanjing. The signs include 'complete goods from the Eastern and Western seas' and 'exchange of money'. Silk scroll of the later Ming period.

27 A Fujian 'Fu' ship of the seventeenth century

reversed many of his father's policies, including those that suppressed the gentry and merchants. Yongle moved his capital from Nanjing to Beijing; in 1403 he built a new city of Beijing, which included the Imperial City and the Forbidden City, expanding the city by four and a half square miles. Once the capital had been moved to the north, the most pressing task was to transport goods to Beijing. Yongle ordered the reopening of the Grand Canal to connect the north and south inland waters. Many important ports sprang up along its banks. Ming dynasty trade became increasingly prosperous as more and more people engaged in commerce. Compared to the first commercial revolution in the Song dynasty, in the second the market economy was broader and economic growth more diversified, providing great resources and capital for maritime trade.[22]

The greatest concentration of markets was in the Yangtze River basin, coastal Fujian and Guangdong, and around Beijing. There was a sharp decline in land ownership, since many people no longer depended on agriculture for their livelihood. Output of cotton increased substantially, with each household growing and processing the crop, and manufacturing cotton goods. The textile industry in both town and country expanded, especially in the region south of the Yangtze, which in time became the centre of the country's cotton-textile production. Many cities and towns, especially along the lower reaches of the Yangtze and Fujian, began to produce special handicraft products, such as various kinds of woven silk, different weights of

paper, and unique earthenware and porcelain. Of the last of these products, the extraordinarily fine blue-and-white porcelain of Jingdezhen and the white porcelain of Dehua in Fujian were sold all over the world.

Maritime navigation and shipbuilding in the Ming dynasty built on the achievements of the Tang, Song and Yuan dynasties and were extremely advanced. The large-scale shipbuilding industry at the beginning of the era was state-run. There were different kinds of ships, including big ocean-faring vessels, warships that fought battles at sea or on rivers, light grain-transporting ships, and fast river vessels. The foremost state-run shipyard in the early Ming dynasty was the Longjiang facility in Nanjing, which covered a vast area. After the ships were built they were launched directly into the Yangtze River. This included the Longjiang Boatyard, where large and advanced seafaring ships had been built for Zheng He's voyages across the western seas.[23]

Chinese seafaring ships started to use compasses for navigation as early as the Song dynasty. Around the twelfth century, compasses invented by Chinese were taken across the seas to Arabia and then through to Europe. China's advanced sternpost rudder can be traced back to the second century, but began to be used by Europeans only in the thirteenth century. Chinese ships already had watertight compartments, which had become increasingly sophisticated by the Song dynasty. The compartments were tightly sealed off from each other so that if one or two started leaking – especially on long voyages across the ocean – water could not flow into adjacent compartments. They were easy to repair and could also be used to keep fish and store fresh water, thus improving the lives of the crew. Starting in Yongle's reign (1402–24), Zheng He (1371–1433/5), who was himself of Arab descent, commanded a fleet of ships on seven diplomatic missions to the West (today's South Seas Islands and the Indian Ocean region). He set out from Suzhou, first sailing to the southern part of Vietnam, and then to West Java, Thailand, Malacca and Sumatra, and thence to Sri Lanka, India, the Moluccas, Aden, Mecca and the east coast of Africa. He visited more than thirty countries in Asia and Africa on these voyages. Zheng He's mission was much earlier than that of Columbus's discovery of the New World of the Americas in 1492.

Columbus had four ships; Zheng He had 317. Columbus's *Santa Maria* was 24 metres long, with a capacity of 250 tonnes. Zheng He's 'treasure ships' were at least 120 metres long, with a capacity of 2,200 tonnes. Zheng He commanded 28,000 men, maritime experts, astronomers and judges. Even Arab interpreters were present on his ships. In total 180 doctors and Chinese medicine specialists sailed on the Chinese ships, as many as Vasco da Gama's entire crew. The scale of Chinese ships – size, crew and equipment carried – was frequently at least ten times greater than that of ships in European fleets. While Columbus's crew were forced to spend their days eating bread cooked with seawater, Zheng He and his crew could enjoy freshwater fish raised in sealed compartments.[24]

From the middle of the Ming dynasty there was a rapid and widespread expansion of the privately owned shipbuilding industry. Ships were designed according to the different circumstances of each shipping route. Famous Ming dynasty ships were the Fujian 'Fu' ship, the Guangdong 'Guang' ship and the Zhejiang 'sand' ship. For example, along the Zhejiang coast there were many sandy shallow waters, so a flat-bottomed 'sand' boat was designed, with a square prow, many masts, fabric sails, and easy to row with oars. Along the Fujian coast, where the wind was strong and the waters deep, the 'Fu' boats were built three storeys high, large enough to hold over 100 people, with two sails, a sharp keel and a wide top.[25] This advanced shipbuilding industry stimulated the development of private overseas trade in the middle and later years of the Ming dynasty. Ming maritime trade was even vaster in scale than the prosperous dealings of the Song dynasty.[26]

Chinese maritime traders had expanded into South East Asia by the early Han dynasty. China's developed agricultural and handicrafts industry and advanced maritime navigation and shipbuilding technology had allowed Chinese merchants to lead maritime trade between the Indian Ocean and the East Asia seas since the Song dynasty. China's maritime trade spread throughout the coastal areas of South East Asia, with long-distance and short-distance trading in commodities such as Chinese silk, porcelain, spices from India and the Malay Archipelago, precious stones from Central Asia, and ivory from East Africa.[27]

TRIBUTE TRADE, PRIVATE MARITIME TRADE AND SMUGGLING

In the early Ming dynasty, maritime links with other countries were strictly banned and foreign trade was conducted mainly through the imperial tribute system. The imperial court had created an extremely rigorous system of regulations regarding tributes and had specifically stipulated the number of envoys and ships from each tribute country. Therefore only tributary missions from foreign countries could obtain permission to enter Chinese ports; it was through these tribute channels that South East Asian countries could obtain Chinese goods. Vietnam, Champa, Korea, Cambodia, Java and other countries offered tribute every three years, Ryukyu every two years, and Japan every ten years. Once the tributary missions arrived in Beijing, they would offer up a fixed amount of foreign goods to the Ming emperor. Under the principle of giving more than receiving, the emperor would then bestow on these envoys all kinds of silk fabrics and goods, often worth many times more than the goods that the envoys had brought in as tribute. If Emperor Hongwu's tribute system

was mainly a diplomatic measure, then Emperor Yongle's method was to exploit the tribute trade to monopolize the country's maritime trade. Zheng He's voyages across the seas represented the pinnacle of the tribute trade and saw the establishment of ports in Vietnam, Java, Sumatra, Sri Lanka and the West Indies.

After Emperor Yongle's death, Zheng He's voyages were brought to an end. In 1433 Zheng He completed his last voyage; he died later that year. The 'treasure ships' were abandoned and fell into decay, and all the documents about the voyages were destroyed. One reason for the change in maritime policy was the rising Mongol threat from the territories in the north. In 1449 the Mongols attacked the Ming and captured the Zhengtong emperor, Zhu Qizhen, at the Tumu fortress, an event which became known in history as the 'Crisis of the Tumu Fortress'. The Ming dynasty turned its attention away from the sea to the interior and the tribute trade began to decline.[28]

Private maritime trade was prohibited from the outset by the Ming government, so at the very beginning this trade was characterized both by commercial activity and by piracy. During the Hongwu era, Japan was plunged into the chaos of civil war. During the seven years from 1368 to 1374 the Chinese coast was harassed by *wokou* (Japanese pirates) on as many as twenty-three occasions.[29] In 1371, in order to prevent anti-Ming forces from colluding with the pirates, the Ming government issued an order that forbade private maritime expeditions and foreign trade. It also restricted the number of foreign merchants coming to China to trade.[30] Whilst the tribute trade had expanded greatly in the Yongle era, especially with Zheng

He's voyages to the west, private foreign trade was now completely banned. Furthermore, there was a strict order that all seafaring vessels should be converted into blunt-headed boats not suitable for long-distance voyages. In the era of Emperor Jiajing it was forbidden to build large boats with more than two masts; all boats that violated this ban would be destroyed.[31] This embargo lasted for over two hundred years.

The direct results of this prohibition on maritime trade were a scarcity of goods coming from China and great profitability for smuggling. The ban on private maritime trade failed to eliminate the harassment from the *wokou*; on the contrary, it stimulated illegal trade at sea. The early period of the Ming dynasty saw every kind of private maritime trade. Some merchants disguised themselves as Ming envoys, or guided foreign merchant ships to smuggling ports along the coast to carry out illegal trade. However, the most common course of action was to risk putting out to sea to transport goods illegally.[32]

Maritime smuggling flourished especially along the south-east coast of Fujian, a region which was surrounded by mountains on three sides, lay far beyond the reaches of imperial power, and had a winding coastline and many bays. Fujian had boasted a maritime trading tradition since ancient times and in the Song dynasty such trade was extremely prosperous. A popular Ming saying was 'The sea is farmland for Fujianese.' Following the maritime ban, boatbuilding was prohibited, and so people's lives were bleak; the only thing one could do was to breach the ban and take up smuggling.

When Fujianese vessels put out to sea it looked as though they were shallow, flat-bottomed boats,

just sailing along the coast. But as soon as they were out of sight of law-enforcement officials they started sailing east and transformed themselves into seafaring vessels: the bulwark was surrounded with a bamboo fence to prevent the waves from rushing onto the deck and a huge knife-shaped wooden rudder was put into the water to stabilize the boat. It took only two days to sail from ports in Fujian to the island of Taiwan, but even this was illegal. According to the law, ships could carry only two days of food and water supplies at most, yet this was enough to allow merchants to enter a whole new world away from Chinese waters. After obtaining further supplies in Taiwan, some merchants might sail along the Ryukyu archipelago as far as the Japanese ports of Hirado and Nagasaki. Others chose to sail along the coast to the Philippines or along the Vietnamese coast to Java.[33]

Private maritime merchants traded with Muslim counterparts and formed the main trading force in the South China Sea region. As early as the second half of the fifteenth century, before Europeans came to the East, China's south-east coast had become the centre of an immense maritime trade region, with Japan lying to the north and the Indonesian archipelago to the south. Although this trading region was not yet global, frequent trade within the region meant that it had achieved a high level of economic integration and become a self-sufficient and highly adaptable international economic system.[34]

The Portuguese and Spanish entered Chinese territorial waters at the beginning of the sixteenth century; together with *wokou* pirates on the south-east coast, they engaged in illegal acts, to such an extent that in the Jiajing era China witnessed a period of soaring piracy.[35] In 1498 the Portuguese

28 A Chinese scroll depicting an encounter with Japanese
pirates, 1555

opened up a new sea route from Western Europe to India. They then took in Goa on the western coast of India and Malacca on the Malay Peninsula, and in 1514 arrived at Tamao Island on the east side of the Pearl River delta in Guangdong in the south of China. In 1552 the Portuguese arrived in the Fujian–Zhejiang coastal areas and engaged in smuggling with the Chinese and Japanese, exchanging Japanese silver for Chinese silk. As a result, the island of Shuangyu developed into a fairly prosperous international smuggling centre.

In the second year of the Jiajing era (1524), due to conflicts among Japanese tribute-bearers, China cut off its official trade with Japan. This led to a rapid development in smuggling, which promised huge profits. Increasing numbers of coastal merchants, small traders, fishermen and farmers became involved in illegal foreign trade. International smuggling in the port of Shuangyu reached its peak in 1544, especially after the return from Kyushu in Japan of Wang Zhi's smuggling ring.

Before the Jiajing era (1522–66), the maritime smuggling trade had been fairly small scale. But during the new era smugglers began to be armed, with smuggling rings possessing great wealth and many ships. On the one hand, they would do business with different places in Japan and South East Asia; on the other hand, they would enter the area between Japan and the Chinese coast, where they would loot, plunder and carry out piratic trade. In the twenty-seventh year of the Jiajing era (1548), after the Ming government had destroyed Shuangyu as a smuggling centre, large-scale piracy shifted to the coasts of Fujian and Guangdong.[36]

29 Song dynasty and Ming dynasty prayers for favourable winds carved into the cliffs at Jiuri Mountain, Quanzhou

Before the Jiajing era it had been mainly Japanese *wokou* pirates who harassed the Chinese coast. But the *wokou* situation became more complicated in the Jiajing era. Apart from those who really were Japanese, most of the *wokou* pirates along the Fujian and Guangdong coasts were Chinese living along the east coast. There were also Malays, Thai, Portuguese, Spaniards and Africans. Most of the *wokou* leaders were Chinese, as were most of their ships.[37] In the forty-fourth year of the Jiajing era (1616), General Qi Jiguang led troops into Guangdong to exterminate the *wokou*. Here he found three main headquarters that were held by local Chinese pirates.[38] The Zhejiang governor Hu Zongxian observed that 'The bandits from the sea nowadays move in their tens of thousands. All say they are Japanese, but actually only a few thousand come from Japan; the others are all Chinese.'[39]

Most smuggling during the Jiajing era took place in the Zhejiang region. By the Wanli era it had shifted to Fujian. Multinational smuggling prevailed mainly on account of the cooperation and support of coastal residents, the local gentry and even Ming officials. All levels of society took part in piracy to one degree or another. Pirates and merchants were interchangeable. When the embargo on sea trade was imposed, merchants were pirates; when it was lifted, pirates were merchants. No wonder the Zhejiang provincial governor Zhu Wan remarked that 'It is easier to get rid of foreign pirates than Chinese pirates; it is easier to get rid of Chinese pirates than Chinese pirates dressed as the gentry.'[40] Faced with the strict Jiajing prohibition on maritime trade, which could implicate a whole clan, some Chinese pirates disguised themselves as Japanese in order to protect their own families. If Chinese army officers and soldiers fighting pirates were defeated, it would be easier to claim this was at the hands of Japanese pirates. If they were the victors, they could gain a higher reward if they claimed that it was Japanese pirates whom they had defeated. So far as the Chinese rulers were concerned, labelling popular unrest along the coast as foreign invasion would make it easier for them to suppress it. Consequently, popular armed rebellion caused by the maritime embargo was treated as foreign invasion.[41] After the death of Emperor Jiajing, the new emperor, Longqing, ratified a lifting of the prohibition on maritime trade, to 'allow trade between east and west seas'. As a result, some of the pirates became lawful maritime merchants and the *wokou* crisis quickly subsided. The *wokou* crisis during the Jiajing era was clearly an extreme expression of the clash between private maritime trade and the government policy that proscribed it.[42]

At the end of the Ming dynasty and the beginning of the Qing dynasty several large and powerfully armed maritime groups, hybrids of trading companies and military forces, appeared along the Fujian coast, led by men such as Li Dan, Zheng Zhilong and Yan Siqi. The most powerful, influential and enduring of these was Zheng Zhilong's group, which became a militant merchant organization, representing the initial incarnation of maritime government.[43]

QUANZHOU AND THE GALLEON TRADE

All sixteen eastern sea routes and the two western sea routes on the Selden map of China started near Quanzhou, connecting this port city on the Fujian coast with sixty ports in the South China Sea region. For the cartographer of the Selden map, Quanzhou

clearly occupied an important position as a big maritime trading port. Quanzhou was situated on the south-east coast of China across the sea from Taiwan, where maritime communication was easy. Proceeding northwards one could reach Japan, Ryukyu and Korea; eastwards the Philippines; and southwards the Malay Peninsula and Java. Quanzhou was the starting point for the 'Maritime Silk Road'. In the Yuan dynasty it was known both in China and abroad as 'the world's greatest trading port'. Many foreign merchants, travellers and missionaries lived there. When Zheng He made his voyages, he had a high regard for the superiority of Quanzhou's port, shipbuilding, foreign maritime trade, goods, religion, talented people, and many other aspects. As there were many Arabs in Quanzhou, Zheng He was able to find the interpreters he needed for his voyages. Quanzhou was the home of sailors, and therefore skilled individuals who understood navigation could be found and recruited. The port was also a collection and distribution centre for silk and porcelain, much of which was taken from there to Western countries. On Jiuri Mountain in Quanzhou there remain to this day Song dynasty inscriptions carved in stone of prayers for favourable winds, as well as more than seventy Ming dynasty inscriptions carved on the cliffs. Foreign trading vessels coming to Quanzhou would arrive with the spring and summer south-east winds, and depart in autumn with the north-west winds. Each year, when the foreign boats hoisted their sails, the Quanzhou magistrate, customs officials and celebrities would climb up Jiuri Mountain to pray for wind for the foreign boats, and would leave behind carved inscriptions.

The Ming prohibition on maritime trade with foreign countries severely affected the development of Quanzhou's economy. The government's attack on private trade forced many merchants to move to nearby harbours that were not so closely guarded, such as the Moon Port at Zhangzhou. In fact, because the ports tended to shift, the map may have rendered navigational launching points offshore vague, not exactly in Quanzhou but rather somewhere between Quanzhou and Zhangzhou, indicating that one would navigate according to circumstances after reaching the offshore destination. In 1567, not long after Emperor Jiajing died, the prohibition on foreign trade was lifted, allowing large numbers of Fujian merchant ships to put out to sea from the Moon Port to carry out legitimate trade abroad. At first the government allowed only 50 Fujian sailing ships to trade in South East Asia. By 1589 this number had increased to 88 a year. By 1592 the number of certificates issued by the authorities for seagoing ships had increased to 110. By 1597 there were as many as 137 legally registered Fujian ships trading at sea.[44]

The galleon trade in Manila was on the rise just at the time the ban was lifted at Moon Port. In 1571 Spain opened up the Servetus (Spain)–Acapulco (Mexico)–Manila (Philippines)–Moon Port (China) galleon trading route.[45] It was mainly Fujian merchants who traded between Manila and the Moon Port. China transported to Manila all kinds of fine silk, coarse silk, raw silk and dyed silk. Silk fabrics included veils, brocades, white silk, coloured silk, printed silk, silk handkerchiefs, velvet, silk stockings, patterned silk parasols and silk–linen blends.[46] These represented the bulk goods traded between China and the Philippines. Antonio de Morga, a Spanish judge in Manila, wrote vividly about the Chinese merchant ships coming to Manila for trade:

The usual practice is that every year a multitude of small boats and big galleons sail from the Chinese Empire to Manila, loaded to capacity with merchandise. Every year about thirty or forty of these boats come. They don't come in one after the other like a big fleet of warships, but in twos and threes. These junks follow the monsoon winds and often come in March when the weather is clear and sunny and the new moon is high in the sky… Their voyage to Manila takes about fifteen to twenty days, and when they have completely sold all their merchandise they sail back at the end of May or beginning of June, before the arrival of the strong south-west monsoon winds, to ensure the safety of their voyage.[47]

When the Chinese arrived in Manila, they congregated to live and trade in the north-east part of the city, known locally as 'raw silk bazaar'. Here, prices were discussed and fixed by the Spanish and the Chinese who were familiar with the market; payment by the buyer was in silver. All transactions had to be completed by the end of May when it was easy for Chinese ships to make their return voyage. At the same time, the Spanish would load their goods onto galleons and transport them to South America before the end of June. The consequence of this, as historians have commented, was that Manila was merely a transfer hub along the silk route between China and South America; so strictly speaking the 'Manila galleons' were galleons transporting Chinese merchandise. So far as South Americans were concerned, the galleons were Chinese vessels; when Spanish Mexicans talked about the Philippines, it was as if they were talking about a province of the Chinese Empire.[48] In 1686 twenty-seven Fujian ships arrived at Manila; by 1709 the trade had reached a high point of forty-three ships.[49]

The Manila trade was the most profitable part of China's foreign trade; it was also the most profitable maritime trading route in the South Seas. Goods transacted were mostly Chinese silk and South American silver. The ban on foreign trade was not completely lifted, however; spurred on by high profits, much smuggling still took place. Smuggling in Manila was especially rampant, and many Chinese sailing ships anchored clandestinely in the vicinity of Manila's port. Many merchants had government shipping certificates to go to Champa, Tokyo, Pattani (in Thailand) or Taiwan, but they secretly slipped into Manila, aiming for a quick exchange of silk for silver. No wonder the Philippines coastline was drawn in great detail and that sixteen ports were clearly marked and named on the Selden map of China.

Porcelain was another big trading commodity in the galleon trade. The main markets for Ming export porcelain were Europe, Japan and South East Asia. In the sixteenth century the Portuguese were the first to come to China and take porcelain back to Europe. In 1602 the Dutch East India Company captured a Portuguese merchant ship, the *Santa Catarina*, which was loaded with a great quantity of Chinese blue-and-white porcelain for export. Not realizing where the porcelain came from, the Europeans named it *kraak* porcelain; in Dutch *kraak* was the word used for Portuguese ships. The next year, this porcelain, which had been produced during the Wanli era in the Ming dynasty, was transported to Amsterdam to be auctioned off. This greatly stimulated the Dutch thirst for Chinese porcelain.

In the seventeenth century the Dutch broke the Portuguese and Spanish monopoly, gaining access to the Chinese porcelain export trade. They commissioned European-style porcelain to be made in China, mostly utensils for everyday use, such as beer mugs and mustard pots, allowing Chinese porcelain to enter ordinary European homes and truly opening up the European market. According to statistics from the Dutch East India Company a vast amount of porcelain was transported by merchant ships from Xiamen to Taiwan or Batavia, and then shipped all over the world via the Dutch East India Company.

Superior Chinese porcelain was highly prized in seventeenth-century Japan, becoming an important component of the Japanese tea ceremony. In 1639 Japan prohibited trade with Portugal and Spain, allowing only Chinese and Dutch ships to dock in the port of Nagasaki to engage in maritime trade. As a result, many Chinese merchant ships went to Nagasaki to compete in trade with the Dutch. Unlike the Europeans with their taste for *kraak* porcelain, the Japanese preferred a special kind of blue-and-white porcelain from Jingdezhen, the so-called 古染付 and 祥瑞, 'auspicious' small porcelain items specifically used in the tea ceremony.

Yamaguchi Prefecture in Japan was not far from the Chinese mainland and Ming merchants would often sail there. In the Yamaguchi Prefecture museum there is a 'Japan–Ming trade ship flag'. On the flag is the family emblem of a Japanese official who managed trade; and beneath this is writing that records that the ship owner of a Ming merchant ship from Quanzhou pledged to return to trade the following year. It also mentions that when the ship arrived the same flag would be raised. This indicates how active Quanzhou's maritime trade was at the time.

In May 2007, the wreck of a Ming dynasty ship, the *Nan'ao I*, was discovered off the coast of Nan'ao Island near Shantou in Guangdong. It had twenty-five compartments and was 27 metres long; it is to date the largest ocean-going merchant ship salvaged in China. Experts have confirmed that this was an armed smuggling vessel from the Wanli era of the Ming dynasty. It is believed that it set out from the Moon Port in Zhangzhou, Fujian, then struck a reef and sank at Nan'ao Island, where the waters of Fujian and Guangdong meet. The ship contained a large quantity of porcelain. So far, more than 6,000 pieces have been recovered, most of which is blue-and-white porcelain from Zhangzhou and Jingdezhen. The discovery of the *Nan'ao I* provides concrete evidence of the Ming dynasty export trade.

Silver was the main currency for the trade between Ming China and other countries. China exported a large amount of silk goods and porcelain, but imported only a small quantity of spices and similar goods. To remedy the trade imbalance, the other side had to pay in money – that is, silver. A great quantity of Mexican silver flowed into China via the Philippines, while the silver smuggled from Mexico to Spain ended up in the hands of the British, French, Dutch and Portuguese. The Portuguese would then transport the silver to the East Indies, and finally it would flow into China. Each year, 2.35 million *liang* (1 *liang* = 38 grams) of Japanese silver could be obtained from Chinese silk traded to Japan. This situation persisted for 250 years, and the huge amount of silver from America and Japan streaming into China became a unique feature of the global economy. Andre Gunder Frank refers to this trade imbalance as 'commercial tribute'.[50]

30 Japan–Ming trade ship flag

A NEW UNDERSTANDING OF THE MING DYNASTY

Maritime trade during the Ming dynasty brought about a collision between East and West. The social, economic and cultural impact of this on the dynasty should not be underestimated. The trade shaped Ming Chinese ideas, lifestyles, political and economic structures, and demographics. It also changed the Western world, contributing to the formation of the global economic system.

The rediscovery of the Selden map has overturned hitherto popular misconceptions about the Ming dynasty and urges us to see China in a very different light. Ming China has often been regarded as a conservative and isolated country. However, the Selden map reveals a relatively open, lively and diverse historical period. It draws our attention to maritime trade in Ming China, China's relationship with other countries at the time, and the social and cultural transformation of Ming society as a whole.

31 A Chinese compass originally kept with the Selden map of China, c. 1650

VALUES, CONSUMPTION, CULTURE

In traditional Chinese society, commerce was insignificant. The social position of merchants was seen as being below that of scholars, farmers and craftsmen. Indeed, they were even suppressed and discriminated against by both the government and society. From the middle of the Ming dynasty the development of commerce and trade brought about a change in social attitudes towards the status of merchants, who gradually rose to occupy a position just below that of scholars. Some people even consider that merchants enjoyed a higher social status. The increasing contact between merchants and literati broke down the barriers between the two groups. Some scholars took on a dual identity of merchant and member of the literati, or abandoned the latter identity altogether; indeed this became a main feature of Ming society. By the late Ming dynasty, a gentry class had begun to emerge, with more and more members of the cultural elite participating in local activities, such as donating to Buddhist temples.[51]

As the population of those engaged in commerce increased, members of the gentry sought to lead cultural trends to maintain their privileged social position. From the middle period of the Ming dynasty onwards, there was a big increase in the consumption of culture and appreciation of fine art and collectibles. Global trade and consumerism in the late Ming dynasty influenced Chinese scholars' tastes in gardens, paintings, books, and so on. Intellectuals and businessmen were actively involved in South China's flourishing art market. The development of artistic tastes and trends was a two-way interaction between scholars and merchants. The scholars needed money to sustain a life of luxury, while the rising merchant class, through the payment of 'tuition fees', sought to develop their taste in art and thereby raise their social status.[52]

The traditional notion of consumption was based on thrift, and at the beginning of the Ming dynasty this continued to be the prevailing idea in society. But from the middle of the Ming this attitude underwent a marked change. In the latter part of the dynasty, global trade and trends in consumption imperceptibly influenced people's attitudes towards daily consumption and lifestyle. A thirst for self-expression and the pursuit of wealth fused together and created extravagant tendencies that engulfed the whole of society. For example, evening banquets no longer offered modest fruit and vegetables, but were now ostentatious displays of meat and fish set out on costly porcelain. The simple four-cornered male headdress ordained by the first Ming emperor was replaced with all kinds of magnificent headgear, and there were bizarrely patterned headdresses for women. Simple cloth shoes were replaced

by magnificent footwear. Rich people's way of life gradually transformed local customs. The extravagance and wastefulness in their etiquette, ceremonies and dress led to a frenzy of showy consumption among the lower strata of society. The Selden map could indeed serve as an example of this kind of conspicuous consumption. Most likely it served as a merchant family's display of its wealth from private maritime trade as opposed to official tributary navigation.

Past dynasties in China had observed an extremely strict hierarchical structure. The basic necessities of life and conduct for different ranks of official and people were regulated by the imperial court. For example, dress and personal adornment were strictly prescribed. People of different status wore different kinds of dress and no infringements of this rule were tolerated. It was still like this at the beginning of the Ming dynasty. By the late Ming, with the development of foreign trade and the abundance of merchandise, people had become tired of the hierarchal dress system and the unsophisticated clothing of the earlier days and they used what they wore to challenge perceptions of their position within society. By the 1560s, gentry and common people alike wore whatever magnificent clothes they wished to wear. Even street vendors dressed resplendently.[53] People also built bigger houses and used better transportation means, which were not permissible for their class according to the state-enforced rules of stratification.

32 Matteo Ricci and Xu Guangqi in an engraving from Athanasius Kircher's *China Illustrata*, c.1667

33 (overleaf) *A Map of the Myriad Countries of the World*, by Matteo Ricci, c.1602

P. Matthæus Riccius Macerat. è Soc. Jesu
prim[æ] Chri[sti]anæ Fidei in Regno Sinarum
propagator.

Lÿ Paulus Magnus Sinarum Colaus
Legis Christianæ propagator.

C c

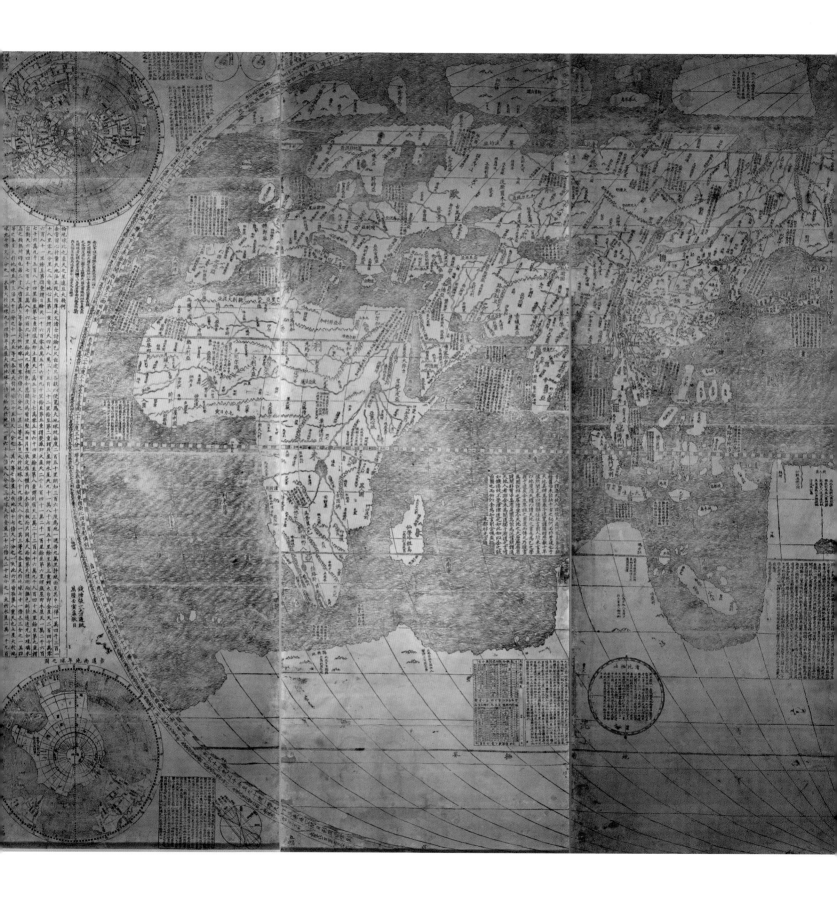

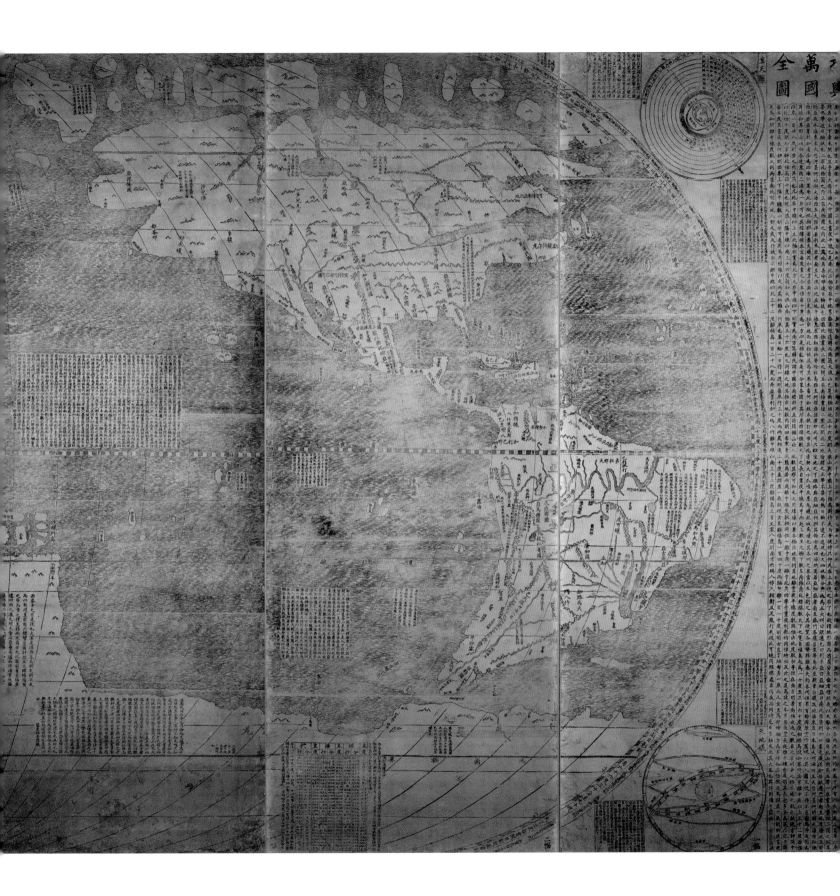

The traditional moral order established by the founding emperor at the beginning of the Ming dynasty also underwent radical change. People travelled everywhere, imaginative ideas flourished and the old taboos were broken. With consumerism driving production, trade broke the moral views formed in an agrarian society, fuelling competition, and in doing so dissolved public norms. The core Confucian values of etiquette, modesty and care for others also disappeared to a great degree. Ming China gradually became a commercialized society where social morality was played down. Some old-fashioned scholars complained that the silver dollar had become the personification of evil and was responsible for bringing China to a state of anarchy.[54]

CATHOLICISM AND WESTERN TECHNOLOGY

From the middle of the Ming dynasty there was widespread penetration of Western culture into China, with the spread of Catholicism and Western science and technology being especially notable. This had a profound influence on many aspects of traditional Chinese culture. Following in the wake of Portuguese and Spanish merchant ships arriving on China's south-east coast were Jesuit missionaries.

Jesuits brought typical Western curiosities such as guns, chiming clocks, spectacles, telescopes and other objects, which had a huge impact on Ming scholars' ideas and concepts of culture. The ingenuity of Western scientific and technological instruments made some of the educated elite realize how advanced Western civilization was and so they began to accept it. Xu Guangqi, Li Zhizao, Li Jingtian, Wang Wei and others were not only fascinated by Western curiosities; they were also

very enthusiastic about the science and technology that lay behind their manufacture. They also translated, together with missionaries, Western science and technology books such as Euclid's *Elements* and an edition of Ramelli's work, *Hydraulic Machinery of the West*, on their own terms.

Xu Guangqi (1562–1633), wanting to make China prosperous and strong, learned from the Jesuit missionary Matteo Ricci, for he wished to introduce Western science, religion and philosophy to traditional culture in China. In the seventh year of the Chongzhen emperor, Xu Guangqi petitioned for the construction of state-of-the-art scientific instruments in order to improve accuracy when producing the imperial calendar. While some literati acknowledged the unique advantage of Western astronomical instruments, they also affirmed the equal status of Western Catholicism and Confucianism, reflecting the propensity towards cultural diversity in their thinking. Since the reign of the Hongwu emperor, the Imperial Astronomical Bureau had established a Muslim division which employed forty-two Muslim scholars; Islamic mosques could be seen everywhere in the city of Beijing.[55]

Matteo Ricci (1552–1610) was a pioneer of Catholicism in China and the first Western scholar who could read and study the Chinese classics. He was respected by many Chinese literati and given the honorific title 'Confucian scholar of the West'. Apart from spreading Catholic doctrine, he also made friends with many Chinese officials and noted public figures. He introduced Western astronomy, mathematics, geography and other scientific and

34 Chinese porcelain depicted in *The Feast of the Gods* by Giovanni Bellini and Titian, 1514/1529

technological knowledge, making an important contribution to the cultural exchange between the West and China. Around 1609 in Zhaoqing, Guangdong, Matteo Ricci used the most advanced map-making technologies, combined with Chinese data, to draw the first Chinese world map the *Shanhai Yudi Quantu* (山海輿地全圖). Later, Ricci drew three more Chinese world maps: the *Yudi Shanhai Quantu* (輿地山海全圖), the *Kunyu Wanguo Quantu* (坤輿萬國全圖) and the *Liangyi Xuanlan Tu* (兩儀玄覽圖). The maps of the world created by Ricci were the most advanced of the time, and helped the Chinese to understand latitude and longitude, the equator, the Tropic of Cancer and other concepts, especially the idea that the world was spherical. He also helped the Chinese to acquire geographical knowledge about the world outside China. Many of the geographical terms and names of foreign places and rivers as translated by Ricci are still used today.[56] He also translated many Western science books into Chinese. Under Ricci's influence, a number of famous Chinese scholars and officials were converted to his religion, including Xu Guangqi.

The cultural exchange between the West and China was mutual. Ricci also introduced Chinese culture to the West. In fact, the data Ricci collected in China not only enabled him to create the most advanced world map at the time, but helped him to prove that the Western name 'Cathay' was indeed the old name used by earlier Western travellers when referring to China.

35 Ewer with Islamic metalwork, traditional Chinese decoration and Portuguese coat of arms, 1522–66

DEVELOPMENT OF BLUE- AND-WHITE PORCELAIN

Blue-and-white Chinese porcelain originated in the Tang dynasty, came to maturity in the Yuan dynasty, and flourished in the Ming and the Qing dynasties. Sold all over the world, Ming Chinese blue-and-white porcelain absorbed cultural elements from abroad and embodied unique artistic styles in terms of colour, shape, pattern and subject matter.

The blue-and-white porcelain of the Yongle and Xuande periods of the Ming dynasty represent the highest quality Chinese ceramics and rank among the most highly prized exhibits in the world's museums. The quality of Yongle and Xuande porcelain is directly related to the voyages of Zheng He. His voyages not only greatly stimulated the production of blue-and-white porcelain, but his ships also brought back the special blue pigment, cobalt, unique to the Middle East that rendered the ceramics distinctively beautiful.

The exotic fine metalware that Zheng He's fleet brought back from the Middle East and West Asia was also an inspiration for Chinese craftsmen in blue-and-white porcelain. Some Muslim traders in China commissioned porcelain to be made in the local style of their own countries, and such styles became extremely popular in East Asian countries. As a result, the blue-and-white porcelain of this period is strongly influenced by Islamic culture in both form and content. Emperor Wuzong converted to Islam, and Islamic decoration appeared on much of the porcelain produced during his reign.

Portuguese traders arrived in China in the sixteenth century and began trading in porcelain. Soon Chinese porcelain led to a European fascination with chinoiserie, influencing trends in

European fashion. Chinese porcelain was often mounted with gold decoration and used for sacred functions. Chinese blue-and-white porcelain can be seen in Giovanni Bellini's 1514 painting, *The Feast of the Gods* (National Art Gallery, Washington DC).

In the course of this exchange between East and West, Chinese-made *kraak* porcelain uniquely blended Chinese and Western styles, as exemplified by the ewer in the collection of the Victoria and Albert Museum in London, which includes Islamic metalwork, traditional Chinese decoration and a Portuguese emblem. A Jingdezhen *kraak* porcelain bowl in the British Museum is decorated with a seven-headed hydra – a Greek mythical monster – and a Latin phrase, *Sapienti nihil novum*, 'To the wise man nothing is new', yet all its other features are typically Chinese. Another example is the *kosometsuke* (古染付) porcelain used in Japanese tea ceremonies. Such vessels were made and decorated in China but based on designs from Japan.

The export of Ming porcelain to Europe gave rise to local imitations of Chinese porcelain, the best known of which is the Delft blue-and-white tin glaze earthenware of the Netherlands. The Netherlands was not the only country to imitate Chinese blue-and-white porcelain; many other countries did the same. The history of the Ming dynasty blue-and-white porcelain trade is that of the interaction between Chinese and foreign cultures.

INFLUX OF NEW FOOD FROM THE NEW WORLD
While Chinese silk, porcelain and tea changed European and American lifestyles, crops from the New World quietly transformed the size of the population and the nature and scale of food production in Ming China. From around 1500 to 1650, the last 150 years of the Ming dynasty, American corn, sweet potatoes, peanuts and tobacco spread to every province in China. These new crops entered the country mainly in merchant ships and through ports along the south-east coast.[57] This sustained an agricultural revolution in the Ming dynasty and created, after 1650, the conditions for a population explosion in China.

After sweet potatoes were discovered in America, they were first planted in the Philippines, from where they spread to the south of China around the middle of the sixteenth century. It is said that Chen Zhenlong, a businessman in Changle County in Fujian, went to the Philippines to do business and brought sweet potatoes back with him to grow in his county. In 1594, when Fujian was suddenly struck by famine, he persuaded the governor Jin Xueceng to get people to grow sweet potatoes to relieve the famine. The sweet potatoes grew quickly and had a high yield. That autumn there was a bumper harvest; there was plenty of food for everyone far and wide, and no one suffered from hunger. As a result sweet potatoes became known as 'golden potatoes'.[58] By the end of the Ming dynasty sweet potatoes were being grown throughout Fujian and Guangdong. Xu Guangqi, close friend of Matteo Ricci and a well-known official scholar at the Ming court, wrote:

> Sweet potatoes … in recent years people abroad had this kind of crop … [It was] brought to Fujian and Guangdong … [S]pread them over the land, plough deep, put thick soil around the base; if there is a serious drought irrigate them with water,

36 Jingdezhen porcelain bowl decorated with seven-headed hydra and Latin phrase, c. 1600–1620

nothing will prevent them from ripening. People from Fujian and Guangdong depend upon these to save themselves from starvation, and the benefit is great.[59]

Between the second half of the seventeenth century and the beginning of the nineteenth there was a sharp increase in China's population. As a result, the need for food also grew. The cultivation of sweet potatoes and corn became increasingly widespread, leading to major changes in land use. These edible crops began to be universally planted because they could be grown on land where it was not easy to grow other crops. This helped to increase the supply of staple foods and support the increased population. Consequently, patterns of food consumption also changed. In some regions sweet potatoes and corn became staple foods, as in the case of the peasants in Ganzhou Prefecture in Jiangxi, where it was said 'the stomach is filled from morning to night with grain, sweet potato and taro, never cooking rice all year round; this has become a custom.' Also in the mountain regions of Hunan it was said that 'in the deep mountains and poor valleys … everyone depends on corn, taro and grains to survive.'

The introduction and cultivation of plant species from abroad during the Ming dynasty also enriched China's culinary arts. Chilli is an extremely important component of Chinese cuisine. It was brought by the Spanish from South America to the Philippines and then traded with Chinese merchants, who brought it into China. Before the sixteenth century, China did not have the chillies of modern times. Today, it is hard to imagine Chinese food without chilli.

THE CHINESE DIASPORA AND HAN CHINESE ASSIMILATION OF TAIWAN

China during the late Ming period was a relatively open society in which many people, especially merchants, travelled widely and settled in various places both within China and overseas. The founding emperor, Hongwu, attempted to set up self-sufficient agricultural co-operatives. The population was not mobile and there were no commercial activities or urban trade centres. All the emperor's subjects had to register their professions with the government, and generation after generation had to engage in the same occupations in the same areas. Despite this stultifying agricultural and financial economic system, Ming society became steadily commercialized. As society stabilized, agricultural production increased and a great number of surplus agricultural commodities appeared. Infrastructure and communication also improved under Emperor Hongwu, facilitating and stimulating private trade and travel.

The emergence of one of China's biggest diasporas occurred during the Ming dynasty, with South East Asia the most important destination. Maritime trade during this period led to a large number of Chinese people, especially Fujianese, migrating to most major ports in South East Asia: Siam, the Malay Peninsula, and Western Java, Manila and Nagasaki. Around 1600, when the Portuguese, Dutch and British arrived in the island regions of South East Asia to buy pepper and other local tropical goods, they discovered that Chinese merchants had already been doing business on the seas of Asia for several centuries. With the development of the galleon trade, many merchants from Fujian gradually settled in the Philippines, where they specialized as trade intermediaries. According to the records of the Spanish colonial government, the number of Fujian settlers in the Philippines increased sharply from only 150 in 1572 to 10,000 in 1588. By 1603, Fujian merchants and workers numbered between 24,000 and 30,000, a much greater total than the 1,200 Spanish and Mexican inhabitants.[60]

Chinese merchants living abroad were scattered over a wide area, ranging from Nagasaki in Japan in the east to Malacca on the southern tip of the Malay Peninsula in the west, covering almost all the important trading ports in South East Asia and the East Asia region. Fujian merchants living overseas brought with them their traditional social ties and networks and re-established these in overseas communities. Well-known local Fujian deities such as the Goddess of the Seas were exported to these communities by Fujian merchants.

The Chinese merchants established special links and relationships with the local authorities and nobility, and became assimilated into the local culture through marriage. In Manila, many Fujian merchants lived in the homes of Spanish priests and Mexican merchants and enjoyed good relationships with their hosts. Each time the Spanish colonial authorities began large-scale expulsions of foreign Chinese residents, the Spanish and Mexican hosts would step forward to protect them.[61] They inter-married with local people, lived among them and had contacts with the upper echelons of society, thus forming a distinct Chinese community. The most flourishing and prosperous Chinese community was that of Fujian merchants who lived in Japan on the north-east coast of the Bay of Hirado. Their activities reached a peak during the period when Li Dan was appointed their leader. Not only did Li Dan

marry a Japanese woman himself; he also helped his adopted son Zheng Zhilong (1604–1661) to do the same – his wife was the biological mother of the Chinese military leader Zheng Chenggong, known in the West as Koxinga.

It is worth noting that Taiwan became part of Chinese territory during the Ming dynasty. Before the beginning of the twelfth century, Taiwan was more or less unknown. Occasionally merchants or fishermen travelling back and forth from the Chinese mainland would sail to Taiwan to take shelter from a storm and trade with indigenous people. It was only between the twelfth and thirteenth centuries that Fujian and Taiwan began to have any real contact. Fujian merchant ships en route to the Philippines would barter with local people. On the voyage south they would usually anchor off the southern Taiwanese coast to replenish supplies of fresh water. In the middle of the sixteenth century when so-called 'Japanese *wokou*' were rampant along China's south-east coast, these pirates actually included many men of Chinese origin and poor fisherman from coastal villages. Hunted by the government, they took refuge in Taiwan and nearby islands.

In August 1604 a Dutch fleet en route to Macau was caught up in a typhoon and drifted towards the Penghu Islands near Taiwan. In June 1622, after failing to capture Portuguese Macau, a fleet of the Dutch East India Company occupied the Penghu Islands instead. In the two years that followed the Dutch did their utmost to force the Ming authorities to open the door to Chinese trade. In August 1624 Li Dan went to the Penghu Islands to act as intermediary in the conflict between the Dutch East India Company and the Fujian authorities. After

much mediation and negotiation the Fujian authorities finally agreed to open up trade conditionally, allowing Fujian merchants to go to Taiwan to trade with the Dutch. The Dutch agreed to leave the Penghu Islands and withdraw to Taiwan.

During the time that the Dutch occupied Taiwan, they built a fortress on the west coast, put down roots and developed the island into an important trading port with China. Fujian merchants quickly changed their traditional sea routes and trading tactics and began to swarm in. Since it was possible to trade tropical goods from South East Asia with the Dutch along the neighbouring Taiwanese coast, many Fujian merchants crossed the strait to Taiwan instead of taking the long sea route to the South East Asian ports. From 1617 to 1624, eighteen of Li Dan's ships went to trade in Taiwan alone. In Beigang, their base in Taiwan, the Li Dan group mustered some three thousand Chinese immigrants, providing them with means of production such as ships, oxen and ploughs, offered them armed protection, and collaborated with the tribal chief to fix boundaries, levy taxes and collect rent from immigrants under their jurisdiction.

Large-scale Chinese migration to South East Asia started in the seventeenth century. In years of war and famine, the Fujian government authorities and the Zheng Zhilong group systematically organized emigration to Taiwan. In the first year of Emperor Chongzhen's reign (1628), when Fujian was hit by yet another famine, the Zheng clan had the support of the provincial governor and collected tens of thousands of famine victims from the

disaster-affected coastal region, gave each person 3 *liang* of silver, and every three people a cow, and transported them to Taiwan to open up virgin territory there. This was the first organized group of migrants to go to Taiwan.[62]

In April 1661, when Koxinga was supporting the Southern Ming regime as a general after the Manchus had established the Qing dynasty, he advanced on Taiwan with 25,000 officers and soldiers and several hundred warships. In February 1662 he forced the Dutch governor general into signing a capitulation. The Koxinga regime brought the Chinese political, cultural and educational system to Taiwan. Great importance was attached to exploiting the land and building water infrastructure, expanding foreign trade and promoting the development of Taiwan's economy. By the final years of the Koxinga regime, the population of Han Chinese in Taiwan had reached 120,000.

MERCHANTS IN COURT POLITICS

In the late Ming and early Qing period, some of the powerful sea merchants began to participate in court politics and thereby played an important role in shaping the political landscape of the empire.[63] Li Dan (d. 1625) came from Quanzhou in Fujian. A famous seventeenth-century pirate and merchant from China's south-east coast, he was a leading figure of the Chinese diaspora. He was originally involved in business in the Philippines, but he did not get on well with the Spanish rulers and so moved to Kyushu in Japan. There, with the help of Japanese pirate groups, he organized a fleet of armed ships. With this fleet he traded with China, Japan and South East Asia (including with the Dutch and the British) on converging shipping routes, and at

37 A commemorative Ming porcelain plate showing the Danby Gate at Oxford Botanic Garden, c. 1755

the same time plundered ships. In his many years of maritime trade, Li Dan not only established good relations with the Japanese feudal lords, but also struck up deep friendships with British and Dutch senior commercial officials stationed in the East. In the last years of the Ming dynasty, owing to his special relationship with the Dutch, Li Dan became a mediator in the dispute between China and the Netherlands, mobilizing the Dutch to withdraw from the Penghu Islands and occupy Taiwan.

After Li Dan's death, his adopted son Zheng Zhilong swiftly took his place. Zheng Zhilong was from Nan'an, Fujian. Not only was he the father of the national hero Koxinga; he was also head of the biggest maritime merchant group at the end of the Ming and beginning of the Qing dynasty. After accepting an amnesty and surrendering to the Ming, he suppressed – on behalf of the Ming government – the pirates who were harassing the south-east coast and frustrated a Dutch invasion at sea. Drawing on support from Ming forces, he eliminated competition and monopolized the maritime trade along the south-east coast. He also forced the Dutch to reach a maritime and trade agreement with him. 'Sea-going ships without the Zheng flag of command would not be allowed to come and go … Fujianese under his protection considered Zheng as the Great Wall.'[64] Zheng Zhilong's business organization began to show the characteristics of a maritime government in its initial stage.[65]

Zheng Zhilong surrendered to the Qing, leaving his maritime kingdom to his son Koxinga. Koxinga, Chinese name Zheng Chenggong (1624–1662), was born in Hirado, Japan, and his mother was Japanese. Koxinga made Xiamen his headquarters and each year sent out fleets of ships to Nagasaki, Taiwan and all the main South East Asian ports to trade. In fact he monopolized the maritime trade of the entire South East Asian region. In 1661, when the Selden map was already in the Bodleian Library, Koxinga, seeking grounds for resisting the Qing, took an army across the sea to recover Taiwan, which had for many years been occupied by Dutch colonizers, and formally established the Zheng armed maritime merchant group as a maritime power. The strict prohibition on foreign maritime contact enacted by the Qing government along the south-eastern coast, aimed at isolating the Zheng clan, had the effect, however, of enabling the Zheng merchant ships to sail to Japan, Siam (now Thailand), Quang Nam (now Vietnam) and other places to purchase rice, grain and other strategic supplies. The Zheng merchant group gained almost complete control of the maritime sea routes to Japan, thus creating an unprecedented rise in foreign trade for Taiwan, until the Zheng clan finally fell.

The Chinese pirate-merchants and their counterparts from Portuguese and Dutch colonial countries competed for control of the eastern and western seas. Zheng Zhilong underwent a complete transformation, turning from the most wanted pirate-merchant into a military general of the Ming court. The Zheng group started with an armed pirate–commercial fleet, but by the end it had annexed Taiwan and exercised the functions of government in the regions it controlled. The entire process of its growth involved mutual support, expansion and interaction, politically, economically and militarily, a phenomenon similar in nature to that of European countries in the thirteenth century.[66]

CHINA ENTERS THE GLOBAL ECONOMY

Although traders from the West entered the markets of the East between the sixteenth century and the early seventeenth, cheap, good-quality Chinese goods were nonetheless very popular in South East Asia and Europe. The Spanish used the cheap silver of the Americas to buy Chinese silk, porcelain and other goods. Chinese traders travelled to Manila to sell Chinese goods and made huge profits. As the Manila galleon trade grew, the numbers of private traders, and countries and regions, involved in the maritime trade increased greatly in South East Asia, and a global trading system began to take shape.

In the late Ming dynasty, silver become China's key import to keep its economy running. The fluctuating exchange rate between gold and silver in Ming China was similar to that of the New World. Europe, South East Asia, Japan, the Ming Empire gradually merged into the nascent world economic system. In the sixteenth and seventeenth centuries Chinese demand for silver, and the demand of other countries for Chinese silk, porcelain and other goods, served to further deepen China's involvement in the world economy.[67]

Batchelor suggests that the shipping routes on the Selden map were connected with the rise of London as a global city. In the 1540s Antwerp in northern European might have been a city with global aspirations, but by the 1700s London, lying on the edge of Europe and the hub of the English wool and cloth trade, would become the centre of the world. Batchelor argues that it was not the much-documented Atlantic trade but the interaction with Asia along the lines traced upon the Selden map that was key to London's modernity.[68]

In the sixteenth century the heart of the world's economy was not yet centred on Europe. It was only several centuries later that the West used the power of technology and narcotics to reverse the trading relationship of China as producer and Europe as consumer. At the beginning of the modern age China's influence on the West was far greater than Europe's influence on Asia. Without the Chinese demand for silver, there would not have been either financing mechanisms for the Spanish Empire or the century-long price revolution which resulted in sudden increases in the rate of inflation between the fifteenth century and the seventeenth in Western Europe. Without China, the birth of world trade would have been delayed for an unquantifiable period of time.[69] In the words of Timothy Brook, 'rather than saying "China's economy is controlled by the tides of the Atlantic Ocean", one could say that the Atlantic tides were pulled by the Chinese moon.'[70]

Given that some scholars assert that world trade was born in 1571 at the beginning of the galleon trade, then it seems fair to suggest that the beginning of world trade should be brought forward to the 1540s – that is, when silver became the main currency in China and China began to seek silver overseas.[71] It was from then on that silver became a world currency through the trading network that almost encircled the globe; as the world's largest economy, China helped form this network. In the Ming dynasty, China played a key role in the initial stages of the construction of a world economic system.

This trading structure based on Chinese goods and Spanish silver connected the Chinese market at the Moon Port with the world market. The network

38 Junks and other Chinese craft sketched by merchant trader Peter Mundy on a voyage to Canton in 1637

of sea routes on the Selden map of China clearly reflects the connection between China and the world and reminds us of China's contribution to the rise of capitalist enterprise in Europe.

The map of Zheng He's voyages is recognized as one of the world's earliest surviving nautical maps. No earlier seafaring map – not even a nautical map of the South Seas – has been discovered. Were the Zheng He map to have been the only seafaring map

to have survived from ancient China, this would have been very unfortunate for the study of ancient Chinese geography, for the history of cartography, and for the Chinese nation.[72] Fortunately, though, after lying concealed from the world for more than three centuries, the Selden map – the earliest large-scale nautical map to survive from the Ming dynasty – finally saw the light of day and filled an important gap in our knowledge. It shows us that China's maritime tradition was not incapacitated by the Ming government's prohibition on this trade. On the contrary, it is now known that as Ming Chinese galleons plied back and forth across the East Asian, South East Asian and South Asian seas, Chinese maritime traders actively participated in the region's commerce, greatly contributing to the global economic system of the seventeenth century.

China and the world were not remote from each other. From the middle of the seventeenth century, China became a part of world history and started to work together with the West in many respects. Ming Chinese society and people's lives underwent huge changes as a result of China's flourishing maritime trade and its active role in the emerging global trade system. The conventional notion regarding Chinese modernity is that China did not start to modernize until the Qing dynasty, when the Qing court was forced to reform when confronted by the threat from the West. To the contrary, the Selden map suggests that China's modernization process had already begun as early as the Ming dynasty.

The Selden map of China has changed forever the world's understanding of Ming China. Ming China was not an inward-looking and isolated agrarian country with little interest in the rest of the world. Rather, the Selden map's web of sea routes connecting China with the world indicates a Ming China that was outward-looking, seafaring and capitalist. China at the time of the Selden map was at the peak of a commercial, lively and pluralistic Ming dynasty.

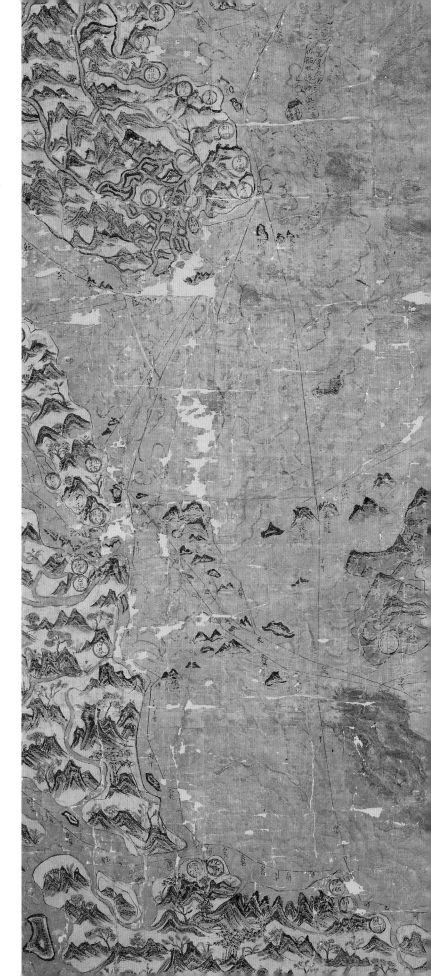

NOTES

1. Interview with David Helliwell, 5 October 2015.
2. Huang Shi-jian (黃時鑒), 'On the Historical Diversity of the "World" Idea in China, Korea and Japan, with Main Discussion of the Korean Cheonhado and the Japanese Nansenbushū Zu' (從地圖看歷史上中韓日'世界'觀念的差異—以朝鮮的天下圖和日本的南瞻部洲圖為主), *Fudan Journal* (Social Sciences) 3, 2008, pp. 30–41; p. 30.
3. Kazutaka Unno (海野一隆), quoted in ibid., p. 31.
4. Liang Erping (梁二平), *Who is on the Other Side of the World: The World Based on Ancient Maritime Maps* (誰在地球的另一邊-從古代海圖看世界), Huacheng Chubanshe, Guangzhou, 2009.
5. Stephen Davies, 'The Construction of the Selden Map: Some Conjectures', *Imago Mundi: The International Journal for the History of Cartography*, vol. 65, no. 1, 2013, pp. 97–105; p. 99.
6. Ibid., pp. 99–100.
7. Robert Batchelor, 'The Selden Map Rediscovered: A Chinese Map of East Asian Shipping Routes, *c.* 1619', *Imago Mundi: The International Journal for the History of Cartography*, vol. 65, no. 1, 2013, pp. 37–63; pp. 37, 42.
8. Guo Yusheng (郭育生) and Liu Yijie (劉義傑), 'Preliminary Analysis on the Completion Date of the Selden Map of China' (東西洋航海圖成圖時間初探), *Haijiao shi yanjiu* (*Maritime History Studies*) 2, 2011, pp. 67–81; p. 81.
9. Yingyan Gong (龔纓晏), 'A Ming Dynasty Nautical Chart Newly Discovered Overseas' (国外新近发现的一幅明代航海图), *Lishi yanjiu* (*Historical Research*) 3, 2012, pp. 156–60; p. 158.
10. Jiarong Chen (陳佳榮), 'The Selden Map of China: A Brief Analysis of Its Composition Date, Features and Overseas Ports' (明末疆里及漳泉航海通交圖：編繪時間、特色及海外交通地名略析), *Haijiao shi yanjiu* (*Maritime History Studies*) 2, 2011, pp. 52–66; pp. 56–8.
11. Jiang Qian (錢江), 'A Mid-Ming Watercolour Navigation Map Recently Discovered at Oxford University' (一幅新近發現的明朝中葉彩繪航海), *Haijiao shi yanjiu* (*Maritime History Studies*) 1, 2011, pp. 1–7, 5.
12. Go Bon Juan, 'Gems of History: The Selden Map of China', 2011, www.kaisa.org.ph/tulay/archive/2010-2011/092011/092011-V24N8.html#gcm.
13. Batchelor, 'The Selden Map Rediscovered', p. 53.
14. Qian, 'A Mid-Ming Watercolour Navigation Map', p. 6.
15. Timothy Brook, *Mr Selden's Map of China: The Spice Trade, a Lost Chart and the South China Sea*, Profile, London, 2013.
16. Batchelor, 'The Selden Map Rediscovered', pp. 55–6.
17. John Selden, *Opera Omnia*, vol. 1, 1726, p. lv.
18. David Helliwell, 'The Bodleian Library's Chinese Collection in the Seventeenth Century', www.bodley.ox.ac.uk/users/djh/UnpublishedPapers/17th.pdf.
19. A.F.L. Beeston, 'The Earliest Donations of Chinese Books to the Bodleian', *Bodleian Library Record*, vol. 4, no. 6 (1953), p. 307.
20. Timothy Brook, *The Troubled Empire: China in the Yuan and Ming Dynasty*, Harvard University Press, Cambridge MA, 2010.

21. Valerie Hanson, *The Open Empire: A History of China to 1800*, W.W. Norton, New York, 2015, p. 378.

22. Ibid.

23. Renchuan Lin (林仁川), *Private Maritime Trade in Late Ming and Early Qing* (明末清初私人海上貿易), East China Normal University Press, Shanghai, 1982, p. 23.

24. Hanson, *The Open Empire*, p. 375.

25. Zheng Ruozeng, 'Chou hai tu bian' (籌海圖編), in Lin, *Private Maritime Trade*, pp. 24–5.

26. Lin, *Private Maritime Trade*.

27. Ibid.

28. Hanson, *The Open Empire,* pp. 360–63.

29. Lin, *Private Maritime Trade,* pp. 50–54.

30. Ming taizhu shi lu (明太祖實錄卷), in Lin, *Private Maritime Trade*; Ming taizhu shilu (明太祖實錄卷), in ibid.

31. Ming taizhu shilu (明太祖實錄卷), in Lin, *Private Maritime Trade*, pp. 70–71.

32. Zhiyu Feng (馮之余), 'Longqing Lifting of the Ban on Foreign Trade and the Growth of Private Maritime Trade', *She ke Zong heng* 2, 2008, pp. 139–41.

33. Yingxing Song (宋應星), 'Chinese Techonology in the Seventeenth Century: T'ien-kung K'ai-wu', in Jonathan Clements, ed., *Coxinga and the Fall of the Ming Dynasty*, Sutton Publishing, Stroud, 2004, p. 13.

34. Brook, *The Troubled Empire*, p. 226.

35. Robert J. Antony, 'The Golden Age of the Chinese Pirates: 1520–1810' (中國海盜的黃金時代: 1520–1810), *Dongnan xueshu* 1, 2002, pp. 34–41.

36. Qing Han (韓慶), 'A Discussion of the Causes of the Ming Dynasty Policy of Banning Maritime Trade', (明朝實行海禁政策的原因探究), *Journal of Dalian Maritime University* (Social Sciences) 5, 2011, pp. 87–92.

37. Kwan-wai So, 'Japanese Piracy in Ming China during the 16th Century', quoted in Antony, 'The Golden Age of the Chinese Pirates, p. 34.

38. Jiguang Qi (戚繼光), 'Qi shao bao Wenji' (戚少保文集), in Lin, *Private Maritime Trade*, p. 44.

39. Hu Zongxian, 'Chou hai tu bian' (籌海圖編), in Lin, *Private Maritime Trade*, p. 42.

40. *Biographies of Zhu Wan* (朱紈列傳, in *History of Ming Dynasty* (明史), vol. 205, quoted in Chen Boyi, 'Disturbance of Trade: "Kou" in the South-eastern Costal Region of China in the 16th–17th Century', *Journal of Port Cities Studies* 4, pp. 3–24; p. 10.

41. Zhi Mo (莫知), 'Pirate Merchants under the Maritime Trade Ban: The Romance of Sea Merchants in the Ming Dynasty' (海禁下的亦盗亦商—明代海商演義), *Haiyang shijie* 9, 2008, pp. 24–9.

42. Fan Shuzhi (樊樹誌), 'Reviewing the "Japanese Pirates", with a Focus on the Japanese Pirates in the Jiajing Period' (倭寇新論，以'嘉靖倭寇' 為中心), *Fudan Journal* (Social Sciences) 1, 2000, pp. 37–46.

43. Ming Wan (萬明), 'Commodities, Merchants and Order: A New Interpretation of the Late Ming Maritime World' (晚明海上世界的重新解讀—商品、商人與秩序), *Gudai wenming* 3, 2011, pp. 76–114.

44. Jiang Qian (钱江), 'Junk Trade, Business Networks and Sojourning Communities: Hokkien Merchants' (古代亞洲的海洋貿易與閩南商人), *Maritime History Studies* 2, 2011, pp. 1–51.

45. Ibid.

46. Fan Shuzhi, 'The Late Ming Dynasty from the Perspective of Globalization' (全球化視野下的晚明), *Fudan Journal* (Social Sciences) 1, 2003, pp. 67–75.

47. Antonio De Morga and J.S. Cummins, *Sucesos De Las Islas Filipinas*, Hakluyt Society at the UP, Cambridge, 1971, p. 305; quoted in Qian, 'Junk Trade, Business Networks and Sojourning Communities', p. 47.

48. Fan, The Late Ming Dynasty from the Perspective of Globalization', p. 42.

49. Qian, 'Junk Trade, Business Networks and Sojourning Communities', pp. 28–9.

50. Andre Gunder Frank, *ReOrient,* University of California Press, Berkeley and Los Angeles, 1998, p. 115.

51. Timothy Brook, *Praying for Power: Buddhism and the Formation of Gentry Society in Late-Ming China*, Harvard University Press, Cambridge MA, 1993. pp. 186–223; Timothy Brook, *The Confusions of Pleasure: Commerce* and *Culture in Ming China*, University of California Press, Berkeley CA, 1999, pp. 210–15.

52. Craig Clunas, *Superfluous Things: Material Culture and Social Status in Early Modern China*, University of Hawai'i Press, Honolulu, 2004.

53. Fang Chen (陳芳), 'A Preliminary Discussion of the Aesthetic Interest in "Weirdness" in the Late Ming Dynasty' (晚明尚'奇'的審美趣味芻議), *Zhuang shi* 11, 2008, pp. 131–3; p. 133.

54. Brook, *The Confusions of Pleasure*, pp. 238–9.

55. Willard Peterson, 'Learning from Heaven: The Introduction of Christianity and other Western Ideas into Late Ming China', in *The Cambridge History of China*, Volume 8: *The Ming Dynasty, Part 2: 1368–1644*, ed. Denis C. Twitchett and Frederick W. Mote, University of Cambridge Press, Cambridge, 1998.

56. Shijian Huang and Yingyan Gong (黃時鑒、龔纓晏),

A Study on Matteo Ricci's World Maps (利瑪竇世界地圖研究), Shanghai guji chuban she, Shanghai, 2004.

57. Huaishuang Wang (王雙懷), 'Crops from Abroad in Southern China in the Ming Dynasty' (明代從海外引入華南的糧食作物), *Collections of Essays on Chinese Historical Geography* 4, 1995.

58. Chen Shiyuan (陳世元), 'Jinshu chuanxi lu', in Lin, *Private Maritime Trade*, p. 375.

59. Guangqi Xu (徐光啟, 'Nong zheng quan shu' (農政全書), in Quan Hanshen, *The Impact of the New World on Chinese Agriculture* (美洲發現對於中國農業的影響) (Studies in Chinese Economic History, vol. 3), Xinya yanjiu chuban she, Hong Kong, 1976.

60. *The Philippine Islands, 1493–1898*, ed. Emma Helen Blair and James A. Robertson, Arthur H. Clark, Cleveland OH, 1903–07, vol. 3, p. 167; Vol. 6, p. 316; quoted in Qian, 'Junk Trade, Business Networks and Sojourning Communities', p. 26.

61. Qian, 'Junk Trade, Business Networks and Sojourning Communities', p. 34.

62. Zongxi Huang (黃宗羲), 'Cixing shimo' (賜姓始末), *Taiwan Historica*, 1995.

63. Ming Wan (萬明), *Commodities, Merchants and Order: A New Interpretation of the Late Ming Maritime World* (晚明海上世界的重新解讀—商品、商人與秩序), 2011.

64. Zou Yiming (邹漪明), 'Ming ji yi wen vol. 4', in Lin, *Private Maritime Trade*.

65. Shunli Huang (黃順力), 'The Rise of Fujian Sea Merchants and Its Influence on the Concept of Oceans' (明代福建海商力量的崛起及其對海洋觀的影響), *Xiamen University Journal* (Social Sciences) 4, 1999, p. 118.

66. Lexiong Ni (倪乐雄), 'The Zheng Chenggong Group and Military-Commerce Compound Theory' (倪樂雄, 鄭成功海商集團與麥尼爾 '軍事 — 商業複合體' 理論), quoted in Huang, 'The Rise of Fujian Sea Merchants', p. 118.

67. Ming Wan (萬明), 'Silver as Currency in the Ming Dynasty: A New Perspective on the Connection between China and the Rest of the World' (明代白銀貨幣化: 中國與世界連接的新視角), *Hebei Academic Journal*, vol. 24, no. 3, 2004, pp. 145–54; p. 153

68. Robert Batchelor, *London: The Selden Map and the Making of a Global City, 1549–1689*, University of Chicago Press, Chicago IL, 2014.

69. Gang Deng, 'The Foreign Staple Trade of China in the Pre-Modern Era', *International History Review*, vol. 19, no. 2, 1997, pp. 253–85.

70. Timothy Brook, *The Troubled Empire: China in the Yuan and the Ming Dynasties*, Harvard University Press, Cambridge MA, 2010, p. 12.

71. Wan, 'Silver as Currency in the Ming Dynasty', p. 152.

72. Liang Erping (梁二平), *Important Ancient Chinese Maritime Maps* (中国古代海洋地图举要), Haiyang Chubanshe, Beijing, 2011, p. 89.

FURTHER READING

Andrad, Tonio, and Xing Hang, eds, *Sea Rovers, Silver, and Samurai: Maritime East Asia in Global History, 1550–1700*, University of Hawai'i Press, Honolulu, 2016.

Antony, Robert, *Elusive Pirates, Pervasive Smugglers: Violence and Clandestine Trade in the Greater China Seas*, Hong Kong University Press, Hong Kong, 2010.

Batchelor, Robert, 'The Selden Map Rediscovered: A Chinese Map of East Asian Shipping Routes, *c.*1619', *Imago Mundi: The International Journal for the History of Cartography*, vol. 65, no. 1, 2013, pp. 37–63.

Batchelor, Robert, *London: The Selden Map and the Making of a Global City, 1549–1689*, University of Chicago Press, Chicago IL, 2014.

Brook, Timothy, *Vermeer's Hat: The Seventeenth Century and the Dawn of the Global World*, Bloomsbury, London and New York, 2008.

Brook, Timothy, *Mr Selden's Map of China: The Spice Trade, a Lost Chart and the South China Sea*, Profile, London, 2013.

Chen, Jiarong (陳佳榮), 'A Brief Analysis of the Composition Date, Features, Route Names, and Names of Places on the Selden Map of China' (明末疆里及漳泉航海通交圖:編繪時間、特色及海外交通地名略析), *Haijiao shi yanjiu (Maritime History Studies)* 2, 2011, pp. 52–66.

Clunas, Craig, 'Things in Between: Splendour and Excess in Ming China', in *The Oxford Handbook of the History of Consumption*, Oxford University Press, Oxford and New York, 2012, pp. 47–63.

Clunas, C., and J. Harrison-Hall, *Ming: 50 Years That Changed China*, University of Washington Press, Seattle WA, 2014.

Davies, Stephen, 'The Construction of the Selden Map: Some Conjectures', *Imago Mundi: The International Journal for the History of Cartography*, vol. 65, no. 1, 2013, pp. 97–105.

Hanson, Valerie, *The Open Empire: A History of China to 1600*, W.W. Norton, New York, 2000.

Lin, Renchuan (林仁川), *Private Maritime Trade in Late Ming and Early Qing* (明末清初私人海上貿易), East China Normal University Press, Shanghai, 1982.

Qian, Jiang (錢江), 'A Mid-Ming Watercolour Navigation Map Recently Discovered at Oxford University' (一幅新近發現的明朝中葉彩繪航海), *Haijiao she yanjiu* 1, 2011, pp. 1–7, 57.

Schottenhammer, Angela, ed., *Trading Networks in Early Modern East Asia*, Harrassowitz, Wiesbaden, 2010.

Schottenhammer, Angela, 'The "China Seas" in World History: A General Outline of the Role of Chinese and East Asian Maritime Space from its Origins to *c.*1800', *Journal of Marine and Island Cultures*, vol. 1, no. 2, December 2012, pp. 63–86.

Yee, Cordell. 'Taking the World's Measure: Chinese Maps between Observation and Text', in *The History of Cartography*, ed. J.B. Harley and David Woodward, vol. 2, pt 2, University of Chicago Press, Chicago, 1994, pp. 96–127.

PICTURE CREDITS

ACKNOWLEDGEMENTS

I would like to thank my colleagues at the Bodleian who helped significantly in various ways at different stages during the process of writing this book. David Helliwell, former Curator of Chinese Collections, introduced the Selden map to me and inspired me to write this book; Joshua Seufert, former HD Chung Chinese Studies Librarian, co-ordinated with Bodleian Library Publishing to have the electronic version of the book published as a printed book. I am grateful to the team of Bodleian Library Publishing, especially head of publishing Samuel Fanous, editor Janet Phillips and picture editor Leanda Shrimpton, whose professional skills transformed the manuscript into a book for a general audience.

I'm also grateful to leading Chinese experts at the University of Oxford and beyond, including Barend J. ter Haar, Run Run Shaw Professor of Chinese; Shelagh Vainker, Associate Professor of Chinese Art and Curator of Chinese Art, Ashmolean Museum; Craig Clunas, Professor Emeritus of the History of Art; Timothy Brook, former Run Run Shaw Professor of Chinese; and Robert Batchelor, Professor of History at Georgia Southern University, who rediscovered the Selden map. I have benefited greatly from their scholarship and insights, either through reading their books or in conversation. I am especially grateful to Robert Batchelor, who kindly agreed to an interview and shared his first encounter with the Selden map, which is narrated in the book.

Special thanks go to Rana Mitter, Professor of the History and Politics of Modern China, Director of University of Oxford China Centre, my mentor and friend, who helped to define the focus at the planning stage of this book.

Finally, I am deeply indebted to my family. Without the sacrifice made by my husband and our two children during the process of the project, writing this book would have been impossible.

INDEX